RORSCHACHIANA XVIII

RORSCHACHIANA XVIII

Yearbook of the International Rorschach Society

Edited by

Irving B. Weiner

University of South Florida Psychiatric Center, Tampa, FL

Hogrefe & Huber Publishers
Seattle · Toronto · Bern · Göttingen

© Copyright 1993 by Hogrefe & Huber Publishers

ISSN 1192-5604

ISBN 0-88937-114-8
Hogrefe & Huber Publishers · Seattle · Toronto · Bern · Göttingen
ISBN 3-456-82350-9
Hogrefe & Huber Publishers · Bern · Göttingen · Seattle · Toronto

Printed in Germany

Table of Contents

Addresses of First Authors

Dr. Irving B. Weiner
University of South Florida
Psychiatry Center
3515 East Fletcher Avenue
Tampa, FL 33613
USA

Prof. Nina Rausch de Traubenberg
Universite Rene Descartes (Paris V)
28 rue Serpente
75006 Paris
France

Dr. Paul M. Lerner
445 Biltmore Avenue, Suite 503
Asheville, NC 28801
USA

Dr. Salvatore Parisi
Scuola Romana Rorschach
Via di Tor Fiorenza, 37
00199 Rome
Italy

Dr. Pilar Ortiz-Quintana
Departmento de Personalidad
Facultad de Psicologia
Campus de Somosaguas
Universidad Complutense
28023 Madrid
Spain

Dr. David Ephraim
Apartado 47581
Caracas 1041-A
Venezuela

Prof. Andre Jacquemin
Department of Psychology
and Education
University of Sao Paolo
Ribeirao, Sao Paolo
Brazil

Dr. Toshiki Ogawa
Institute of Psychology
University of Tsukuba
Tsukuba, 305
Japan

Dr. Carl-Erik Mattlar
Sporrgatan 8 F 79
SF-20880 Turku
Finland

Dr. Jan J. L. Derksen
Twaalf Alpostelenweg 2
6523 LW Nijmegen
The Netherlands

Dr. Philip Erdberg
21 Tamal Vista Boulevard,
Suite 125
Corte Madera, CA 94925
USA

Speaking Rorschach:
A Tower of Babel No Longer

Irving B. Weiner

University of South Florida Psychiatry Center, Tampa, FL, USA

The book of Genesis tells about a time when all the peoples of the earth spoke the same language and had come together to build a tower that would reach into heaven. As punishment for this vanity, people were "scattered abroad" and their language was "confounded," so that they could no longer understand one another's speech. The unfinished tower was called "Babel," and "Tower of Babel" has since come to signify poor communication among people whose language differences prevent them from understanding each other.

The history of the Rorschach test has proceeded through its own Tower of Babel. From its beginnings in Switzerland as a German language instrument (Rorschach, 1921/1942), the test soon spread into worldwide use in many different languages. Over the years many distinctive ways of using the Rorschach were developed in individual countries, and numerous productive lines of investigation emerged. For a long time, however, Rorschach clinicians and researchers around the world were for the most part only faintly aware of the work that was being done with the test in countries other than their own or what was being written about it in languages other than their own.

Technological advances in travel and communication have shrunk the world in which we live, and the national separatism of professional persons interested in the Rorschach has gradually given way to international camaraderie and information exchange. Central to this escape from isolation have been 13 Congresses sponsored by the International Rorschach Society. Since the first of these congresses was held in Zurich in 1949, these international meetings have become increasingly well-attended and broadly representative. The XIII International Congress of Rorschach and Other Projective Techniques in Paris in 1990 attracted over 650 participants from 31 different countries. The extensive sharing of facts and opinions that occurred during the Paris congress bore witness to how far we have progressed in surmounting problems in communication that once interfered with our learning from each other.

The establishment of *Rorschachiana* as an annual journal of contributions from around the world is a significant new step in enhancing global communication about the Rorschach. The articles appearing in the journal will call special attention to how the Rorschach developed and how it is being used in various countries. In time, it is hoped, every country in which Rorschach assessment is being practiced or studied will be represented by contributed articles.

With respect to the Tower of Babel, clinicians and scholars everywhere should recognize that in speaking Rorschach, they speak an international language. Like musicians who can join colleagues in performance anywhere in the world and read the music with authority, so too can Rorschachers read a test protocol intelligently wherever they may be. Shown a protocol with an Erlebnistypus of 6:3, for example, a Rorschach clinician anywhere can be reasonably certain the subject is a person who generally prefers thought to action and who typically responds to situations in an ideational rather than an expressive manner.

The universality of Rorschach language is not challenged by the existence around the world of different systems for coding responses and different approaches to orchestrating the interpretive process. Communication does not require agreement, nor is the adequacy of communication measured by whether agreement results. The Rorschach can be used effectively in many ways, and any way that proves effective merits respect. It is as Sigmund Freud (1904/1953) wisely said about treatment: "There are many ways and means of practicing psychotherapy. All that lead to recovery are good" (p. 259). What communication requires is understanding, and, if Rorschachers are able to understand each other's native tongue, whether through translation or by virtue of multilingual abilities, they can discuss their views about the test with clear understanding.

And so we begin, with contributions in this first issue from Brazil, Finland, France, Italy, Japan, The Netherlands, Spain, the United States, and Venezuela. As Editor, I am honored to have been given the opportunity to bring together international wisdom concerning the Rorschach, and I invite readers of *Rorschachiana* to guide me with their comments and suggestions.

Irving B. Weiner

Résumé

Le livre de la Genèse Parle d'une époque à laquelle tous les gens de la terre parlaient la même langue et se rassemblèrent pour construire une tour, qui atteindrait le ciel. Punis de leur vanité, ils furent disséminés "à l'étranger" et leur langue fut "confondue", afin qu'ils ne puissent plus se comprendre. La tour inachevée fut appelée "Babel" et l'expression "Tour de Babel" en est venue à désigner une piètre communication entre des personnes dont les différences de langue les empêchent de se comprendre.

L'histoire du test de Rorschach a connu sa propre Tour de Babel. Après ses débuts en Suisse, comme instrument en langue allemande (Rorschach 1921/1942), le test devait rapidement s'étendre à une utilisation mondiale dans bien des langues différentes. Au cours des années, des utilisations distinctes du Rorschach se développèrent dans plusieurs pays et de nombreuses voies d'investigation émergèrent. Toutefois, les cliniciens et les chercheurs du Rorschach ont eu longtemps une connaissance très limitée des travaux qui se faisaient dans d'autres pays que le leur ou qui s'écrivaient dans des langues autres que la leur.

Les progrès technologiques en matière de voyage et de communication ont rétréci le monde dans lequel nous vivons et le séparatisme nationaliste initial des professionnels du Rorschach s'est progressivement mué en une camaraderie internationale et un échange d'informations. Au coeur de cette rupture hors de l'isolationnisme figurent les 13 congrès parrainés par la Société Internationale de Rorschach. Depuis le premier congrès, qui se tint à Zürich en 1949, ces rencontres internationales sont devenues de plus en plus fréquentées et de plus en plus représentatives des divers courants. Le XIIIème Congrès International du Rorschach et des Méthodes Projectives, à Paris en 1990, attira plus de 650 participants de 31 pays différents. L'étendue du partage d'observations et d'opinions, qui s'y déroula, vient témoigner de notre capacité croissante à surmonter les problèmes de communication qui, jadis, empêchaient que nous apprenions les uns des autres.

L'instauration de "Rorschachiana" comme revue annuelle, regroupant des communications du monde entier, représente une étape significative pour accroître la communication globale autour du Rorschach. Les articles publiés dans la revue se centreront plus particulièrement sur l'évolution du Rorschach et sur son utilisation dans divers pays. Avec le temps, nous espérons que chaque pays, où se pratique et s'étudie le Rorschach, soit représenté par des contributions d'articles.

3

Pour en revenir à la Tour de Babel, cliniciens et érudits de partout devraient reconnaître qu'en parlant Rorschach, ils parlent un langage international. Tels des musiciens qui peuvent se joindre à des collègues en concert, n'importe où dans le monde, et lire les notes avec assurance, les Rorschachiens, de même, peuvent lire un protocole intelligemment, où qu'ils se trouvent. Par exemple, devant un protocole avec un Erlebnistypus de 6 : 3, un praticien du Rorschach, n'importe où, peut être raisonnablement certain que le sujet est une personne qui préfère généralement la pensée à l'action et qui, typiquement, répond à des situations sur un mode idéationnel plutôt qu'expressif.

L'universalité du langage Rorschach n'est remise en question ni par l'existence de différents systémes de cotation des réponses, ni par la diversité des approches qui orchestrent le processus interprétatif. En effet, communiquer ne signifie pas nécessairement "tomber d'accord", car l'adéquation de la communication ne se mesure pas à l'émergence d'une entente. Le Rorschach peut être utilisé efficacement de plusieurs manières et toute manière, qui se démontre efficace, mérite du respect. Comme le disait sagement Freud (1904/1953), à propos du traitement: "Il existe de nombreuses manières et moyens de pratiquer la psychothérapie.… Toutes celles qui mènent à la guérison sont bonnes" (p. 259). Ce que requiert la communication, c'est la compréhension; si les Rorschachiens sont en mesure de comprendre la langue maternelle de chacun, que ce soit par le biais de la traduction ou de leur propre capacité à être polyglotte, ils peuvent discuter alors de leurs opinions sur le test avec une compréhension claire.

Ainsi, nous commençons cette première parution avec des contributions du Brésil, de l'Espagne, des Etats-Unis, de la Finlande, de la France, de l'Italie, du Japon, des Pays-Bas, et du Venezuela. En tant que directeur de publication, je suis honoré d'avoir reçu l'opportunitè de réunir la sagesse internationale en matière de Rorschach, et j'invite les lecteurs de "Rorschachiana" à me guider par leurs commentaires et leurs suggestions.

Resumen

El libro del Génesis cuenta acerca de un tiempo en el cual todos los pueblos de la tierra hablaban el mismo idioma y se habian juntado para construir una torre que llegara hasta el cielo. Como castigo por su vanidad, los pueblos fueron "dispersados" y sus lenguajes "confundidos", de manera de que no pudieran entenderse más unos con otros. La torre inacabada se llamó "Babel", y, desde entonces, "Torre de Babel" ha venido a significar la mala comunicación entre los pueblos, cuyas diferencias de lenguaje les impide entenderse unos a otros.

La historia del Rorschach procedió a través de su propia Torre de Babel. Desde sus comienzos en Suiza como un instrumento en idioma alemán (Rorschach, 1921/1942), el test se expandió rápidamente por todo el mundo, y en muchos idiomas diferentes. Con el paso de los años, se desarrollaron en distintos paises muchas modalidades diferentes de usar el Rorschach, y emergieron numerosas lineas productivas de investigación. Por un largo tiempo, sin embargo, los clinicos e investigadores del Rorschach alrededor del mundo eran, en su mayor parte, apenas conscientes del trabajo que se venia realizando con la prueba en paises diferentes al propio, o de lo que venia siendo escrito en otros idiomas.

Los avances tecnológicos en el transporte y la comunicación han encogido el mundo en el cual vivimos, y el separatismo nacional de los profesionales interesados en el Rorschach ha cedido el lugar a la camaraderia internacional y al intercambio de información. Trece Congresos, patrocinados por la Sociedad Internacional de Rorschach, han sido centrales en este escape del aislamiento. Desde que el primero de tales congresos fué realizado en Zurich, en 1949, estos encuentros internacionales han venido incrementando su asistencia y representatividad. El XIII Congreso Internacional del Rorschach y Otras Técnicas Proyectivas, realizado en Paris en 1990, atrajo a más de 650 participantes de 31 países diferentes. El intercambio extenso de hechos y opiniones que tuvo lugar durante el congreso en Paris testimonia cuánto hemos progresado en sobreponernos a los problemas de comunicación, que una vez interfirieron con la posibilidad de aprender unos de otros.

Un nuevo y significativo paso en el estimulo a la comunicación global en torno al Rorschach lo constituye el que *Rorschachiana* se haya establecido como una publicación anual con contribuciones alrededor del mundo. Los articulos que aparezcan en la revista prestarán especial atención a cómo el Rorschach se ha desarrollado y está siendo usado en diferentes paises. En su momento, eso esperamos, estarán representados, a través de sus contribuciones en articulos, todos aquellos paises en los cuales el Rorschach esté siendo practicado o estudiado.

Con respecto a la Torre de Babel, los clinicos y estudiosos del Rorschach en todas partes deberian reconocer que al hablar en Rorschach, están hablando un lenguaje internacional. Al igual que los músicos, los cuales pueden ejecutar con sus colegas en cualquier parte del mundo y leer la música con autoridad, igualmente pueden los Rorschachistas leer inteligentemente un protocole del test, dondequiera que se encuentren. Frente a un protocolo con un Erlebnistypus de 6:3, por ejemplo, un clinico del Rorschach en cualquier parte puede estar razonablemente seguro de que el sujeto es una persona que prefiere, por lo general, el pensamiento a la acción, y de que responde tipicamente a las situaciones de una manera más ideacional que expresiva.

La universalidad del lenguaje del Rorschach no se contradice con la existencia, alrededor del mundo, de diferentes sistemas para codificar las respuestas y diferentes enfoques para orquestar el proceso de interpretación. La comunicación no requiere el acuerdo, ni lo adecuado de la comunicación se mide por si se ha llegado o no a un acuerdo. El Rorschach puede ser usado efectivamente de muchas maneras, y cualquiera de ellas que se demuestre efectiva merece respeto. Como Sigmund Freud (1904/1953) expresó sabiamente respecto al tratamiento: "Hay muchas formas y medios de practicar la psicoterapia. Todo lo que conduzca a la recuperación es bueno" (p. 259). Lo que la comunicación requiere es comprensión, y, si los rorschachistas son capaces de entender la lengua materna del otro, ya sea a través de la traducción, o en virtud de su conocimiento de otros idiomas, pueden discutir sus puntos de vista acerca del test con una clara comprensión.

Y asi comenzamos, con contribuciones, en este primer número, provenientes de Brazil, Finlandia, Francia, Italia, Japón, Holanda, España, Estados Unidos y Venezuela. Como Editor, me honra el que se me haya dado la oportunidad de reunir sabiduria internacional acerca del Rorschach, e invito a los lectores de *Rorschachiana* a guiarme con sus comentarios y sugerencias.

References

Freud, S. (1904/1953). On psychotherapy. *Standard Edition* (Vol. VIII; pp. 257–270). London: Hogarth: 1953.

Rorschach, H. (1921/1942). *Psychodiagnostics*. Bern: Hans Huber.

The Rorschach: From Percept to Fantasm

Nina Rausch de Traubenberg

Université René Descartes, Paris, France

Recently I was asked to select from my various papers on clinical psychology the one I preferred and in which I expressed most clearly my approach as a clinical psychologist. This led me to think about what has been the main theme of my research, clinical practice, teaching activities, and scientific papers. I would like to call this theme a sensitivity toward all that is interactive and linking. This sensitivity, initially intuitive, became a systematic search for relationships and interactions.

Looking back at the various steps in my professional as well as personal life, I came across this sometimes obvious, sometimes hidden framework. My personal motivation could not have been better served than by the Rorschach, a sensitive test capable of revealing many such links. This could be reversed, however, and I could equally well propose that I became aware of this personal motivation through the Rorschach.

Are we really entitled to look for a link between the choice of our working tool and of our internal attitude? I think that it is worthwhile to do so, each of us for himself or herself, just as it is important to maintain awareness of the role played by our intuition in data interpretation, because this intuition complements scientific competence.

Finally, I chose as my preferred paper the lecture I gave during the X International Congress of Rorschach and Projective Methods in Barcelona, published later in France under the title "The Rorschach, a Space for Interactions" (1985). I would like to devote these pages to the presentation and development of this theme.

Background

The Rorschach as a "space for interactions" is a formula that came to my mind in the course of my research on children's reactions to the Rorschach Test. This expression seemed to me to account very well for the nature of the Rorschach as not only a simple visual stimulus, but also as a space in which complex psychological processes occur.

The response process involves the mobilization of various functions, starting with perceptual activity, but subsequently including imaginary and even fantasy activities as well. It is the product of this complex set of processes that we analyze; that is, we analyze not only *what* is said but also *how* it is said. In other words, a meaning or significance is given to these visual stimuli that is, to be sure, an objective reality, but that is nevertheless created in such a way that it harks back to another reality, an internal reality shaped by fantasy. What is experienced by the subject confronted with the blots varies greatly, running from simple description of an objective reality to the most subjective and/or the most unreal imaginary experience.

The specificity of the Rorschach as a system of interactions, as a space in which various psychic movements occur, is revealed with respect to the following considerations:

1. *The circumstances of the Rorschach test situation.* Whether in response to implicit features of the test situation or explicit instructions, the patient-examiner relationship creates a framework in which threads of objectivity and subjectivity mingle.
2. *The stimulus.* All of the inkblots are symmetrical, arrayed on either side of a vertical median axis, thus creating a spatial rhythm that Rorschach judged essential. The objective characteristics of the inkblots include their shapes, colors, shadings, and figure-background relationships. These perceptual qualities are discussed in detail by Schachtel (1966). The stimulus emerges as compact or scattered, as stable or unstable, as precise or vague, as massive or delicate, and above all, as constructed but not finished, complete or incomplete, and full or hollow. Young children, for example, organize the stimulus in relation to their own body, that is, they project their body on to it. Very ill adult patients do likewise. Thus, Card V becomes for a 5-year-old boy with a congenital heart disease "an operated-on heart" and for an 8-year-old boy with a kidney disease "an ill rabbit, a dead rabbit – a healed rabbit."

Integrating these characteristics generates hypotheses concerning the potential symbolic value of the stimulus and its pull. This value is never limited to a single meaning, but rather depends on the level of psychic functioning on which the subject is reacting, whether on a primary regressive level or an adaptive and inventive secondary level.

3. *The instructions.* Although referring to well-defined stimulus objects, the instructions that are given ("What might this be?") invite an infinite number of possibilities that, as noted by Schafer (1954), run from percept to fantasy.

4. *The response.* Rorschach (1921) proposed a three-part scoring of the response ("what is said"). In so doing he asserted the importance of an interaction: he brought together in a single formula the space (location), the way in which this space is experienced (determinant), and how subjects place themselves in it (content). The image in its frame is an object of knowledge either acting or acted upon. Therefore what is perceived and what is experienced are co-mingled. Put differently, perceptual activities are personalized. No one has given a better definition of behavior and attitude toward the Rorschach Test than Daniel Lagache, who in 1957 distinguished between "perceptual activity" and "fantasy activity" and asserted that only the latter fits responses to the Rorschach Test blots.

The three elements of scoring are important because they show the relationships among the expressed need, the strength of conflicts, the flexibility or rigidity of defenses, and the movement between regression and reconstitution. However, the meaning of the scores should be related to the manner in which the response is given, the location of the response, the card to which it is given, the color of the stimulus area used, whether the response is given in the beginning or at the end of the test, and the manner of expression. French psychologists and psychiatrists have been particularly interested in language and verbalization. Minkowska (1956) and her group tried to establish a relation between the style of verbalization and the subject's mental structure. Cosnier (1969) proposed concepts and methods for a psycholinguistic approach to the Rorschach. He argued that the classical approach to scoring content tended to lose three-quarters of the testee's message. How subjects express themselves in giving Rorschach responses can be assessed directly by analyzing grammatical errors or errors in logical thinking that occur even when word usage is appropriate. Thus, Merceron, Husain, and Rossel[1] recommend a type of discourse analysis which is based upon Piaget's genetic theory.

9

These qualitative components are very difficult to objectify, and yet they can be decisive. The diagnostic use of the Rorschach test is too often based only on formal data, i.e., quantitative data such as frequencies, without considering qualitative data, the markedly empirical character of the method, or the variety of psychopathological models, and also without considering the extreme creativity of the author who repeatedly revised his thinking in accordance with new developments.

5. *The interpretive value of the scores.* The interpretive hypotheses suggested enthusiastically by Rorschach were empirical, and, as he said himself, they have a transient character. He called for further study of the "reciprocal game" of factors. The interpretive value of the scores is not in fact unequivocal. Consider the following features of the form level and of color and human movement responses.

Form reflects recognition of objective reality, but it may have an affective connotation as well, as in the case of Schachtel's "dynamic" Fs, which occur so often in children's Rorschachs. There are many different ways of "mastering the chaos" when one considers Mayman's very refined classification of the forms (1970). More recently the form has been viewed as an outline, an envelope, a way of delineating the outside from the inside (Chabert, 1983).

Color responses reflect various meaning depending upon the color itself (red, grey, black, white, pastel), the location, the content, and the feeling tone. What is more difficult to handle than the color on the Rorschach? There are many varieties of "affect" or of experiencing affect as well as the elaboration of sensory experience. Sum C as a simple frequency of color responses is not only insufficient but completely misleading; it leads to an absurd mixture of destructive contents, regressive movements, passive receptiveness, narcissistic needs for valorization, interpersonal needs, and needs for emotional involvement. Obviously, color responses cannot have an unequivocal affective meaning.

Human movement responses have the most diverse and least unequivocal interpretive value, given the richness of their implications. Contradictions are obvious between authors who translate the Rorschach in terms of external behavior and those who consider Rorschach responses as mental attitudes and aspects of fantasy life. In my opinion the projective aspect becomes essential here, as is the reference to body schema. The human response can be interpreted in terms of identification and empathy, of cathexis of thought, or of a distancing from the action in reference to the body as an organizer, whether in accurate or

10

poor form, whether real or unreal, whether sexualized or not, and whether depicting a posture or relationship. The movement responses are often the most direct expression of elaborate fantasy scenarios. A more current interpretation examines the movement response in terms of self-representation and self-relationship, in which the self is either locked in the boundaries of the perceived or dispersed and projected in the external world. Consequently a precise analysis of each movement response is necessary before deciding on its particular meaning.

For the past 15 years the meaning of movement responses has been enriched by such considerations. The human response has been the object of multidimensional analyses in which these human representations are used to assess the quality and level of object representation (Blatt, 1976) and even of object relationships (Mayman, 1967). Mayman refers primarily to psychoanalytic theory in his exclusive attention to the contents of the test, whereas Blatt examines aspects of process as well and integrates the cognitive developmental theories of Werner (1940) and Piaget (1937) with psychoanalytic perspectives. Lerner and Lerner (1980), in analyzing primitive defense mechanisms such as splitting, denial, idealization, projective identification, also make extensive use of human figure responses.

Human responses take a prominent position – perhaps too much so – in test interpretations framed in psychoanalytic theories focused in particular on the development of object relations and the process of internalization of experiences (Mahler, 1975; Fairbarn, 1952; Winnicott, 1975). A number of authors give special status to movement responses, already termed as "Salz in Suppe," and consider them to be the noble element in a Rorschach protocol. But what then is one to do with protocols without any or with only one movement response, of which there are many? It is necessary to strike a balance and attend to such elements as animal, botany, and inanimate contents that may in fact be substitutes for human representations. Such a balance was proposed, though in a different perspective, by M. Orr (1958), then by Rausch de Traubenberg and Sanglade (1984) in Europe and by Ipp (1986) in the U.S.

Discussing the interpretation of the Rorschach scores calls for comments on the methods of analysis and modes of interpretation practiced in the Institute of Psychology in Paris. Analyzing protocols, we take into account the Rorschach test situation, for us a very special situation that combines a call to dreaming and to free expression while observing an external objective reality, that of the relationship and of the object. The testing situation must help subjects express what they are unable to say

11

clearly, and it must not push them to say what they do not want to. Opportunity for free expression and even for play is thereby provided. Nevertheless, subjects may perceive being tested as a burden, and they are likely to regulate their choices with each card and according to their needs to express or to resist expressing their attitudes, conflicts, and wishes. For us this is the route to follow in order to appreciate the complexities of the fluctuations between reality and fantasy.

Clinical Research

Percept-Fantasm Interactions in the Rorschach Test in Children

Our research on pre-psychotic organization in children enabled us to systematize the concept of interferences between perceptual and fantasy activities in children's Rorschachs. It is well known (Engel, 1963; Rausch de Traubenberg & Boizou, 1980; Rausch de Traubenberg et al. 1973) that in borderline children there is a back and forth movement between an archaic world of drives and a more socialized world. The intensity of fabulation and of fantasmatic experiences does not hinder a rapid recovery; although fragile, the perceptual and cognitive framework remains cathected. Beginning with this observation, we have re-examined the protocols of 260 children from eight clinical and three non-clinical groups. The purpose was to examine the interaction between the use of a perceptual framework and the expression of the needs. In other words, it was to define how the percept is influenced by the affective pressure or, alternatively, to define the reparative role of perceptual elements in the face of obvious fantasmatic pressure.

By setting up a grid, it was possible to assess the various interactions among perceptual approaches and the level of associations. When a deterioration occurred, the card, determinants, content, and underlying unconscious theme were all noted. We also noted how reconstitution came about, through which expressions, formal or not, and in what mode. The most difficult to appreciate is the degree of oscillation between progressive and regressive responses, even though this is what should be used for a prognosis.

Four types of interference have been catalogued, three with various degrees of deterioration and one in which, by contrast, mental processes were used to express a conflict.

12

The significance of this research lies in having highlighted the role of fantasy as an *organizer*, in contrast to its more well known destabilizing role. In this latter case resources are suddenly mobilized with the greatest intensity as if the fantasmatic drive compelled subjects to deviate from their usual ways of functioning. This hyperarticulation is not always a sign of precocious maturity; rather it is often a kind of creative explosion that may happen only once in the test. Generally the configuration of the blot confirms where this occurs, the obvious theme being presented in a well-articulated scenario.

These researches enabled us to propose a theoretical model for the interpretation of children's Rorschachs, in terms of *interferences between perception and fantasy*. No only does this model account for the specificity of children's Rorschach, it facilitates the interpretation of protocols in other clinical settings as well. Our clinical experience also suggested the hypothesis that *the intensity of conflict, the need for expression, and the need for achievement are reflected both at the mental and perceptual level and at the intrapsychic and affective levels.*

Percept-Fantasm Interactions in the Rorschach Test in Adolescents and Adults

The combined reference to percept and fantasy makes it possible to determine a level of psychic functioning that is equated with a psychiatric diagnosis. In the Rorschach Test perceptual and fantasmatic activities are not differentiated within the response, but are intermingled in the response process, a process akin to play, a play due to an image-making behavior or to the "unlocking of the book of the private imagery" (Schafer 1954). For a long time these two types of activity were analyzed separately, sustaining the controversy between adherents to formal scores and to thematic data.

We are all familiar with the emphasis given by many authors to the perceptual components of the Rorschach and to the choice of determinants. At the same time, everyone knows how difficult it is to prove the validity of so-called structural indicators as nosological signs. Some researchers have emphasized the *perceptual aspect* in isolation, analyzing it in terms of levels of development and nosological meaning. One should recall the remarkable researches of Friedman (1953), Hemmendinger (1960), and Dworetzki (1939) in which the levels of perceptual organization are translated into stages of regression of mental illness and compared to the developmental levels of perception in the child. Perceptual modes have been related to specific modes of thought, such as obsessional or paranoiac. *The motivational, fantasy aspect* has also been studied in isolation through determinants and even further through contents. Various foci such as body boundaries, self representation, libidinal drives, aggressive drives, and defense mechanisms have been examined.

Some authors have attempted to consider both activities together in order to achieve accurate diagnosis in the adult clinical field. Zulliger (1949) had already suggested a relationship between apperceptive modes and stages of libidinal development. I wish to stress the impressive pioneering work of Bower, Testin, and Roberts (1960) that combines thought processes, expressive style, and contents in specially constructed scales. The authors use psychoanalytic concepts as reference points but do not limit themselves to analysis of content. On the contrary, they conclude that it is necessary to combine the two types of scores to obtain sufficient data for diagnostic purposes and to assess the level of ego functions and object relations.

In the clinical field, the most satisfactory effort to link perception and fantasy in Rorschach interpretation as proposed by Schafer in 1954. He observed the underlying factors of the responses and their sequence and from that he deduced the levels of the psychic functioning and the mode of articulation among drive, defense, and adaptation.

In short, is it possible to characterize percept and fantasm, external and internal realities, as two separate objects of research, the object of psychoanalytic research being fantasm and the object of psychological research being behavior? For the Rorschach test, this division is artificial and even incongruous, because the Rorschach's value lies precisely in the simultaneous call for both to create meaning! Extreme cases in which subjects show too great a fixation to one of these poles, perceptual or fantasmatic, demonstrate deviance in the form of either a complete break with fantasy or a complete invasion by it. The latter is associated with mental pathology, whereas the lack of fantasy is most commonly observed in psychosomatic patients and in non-patients. This could be expected because, as is known, fantasmatic activity is mobilized by psychic trauma, conflicts, and pain.

14

Percept-Fantasm Interactions: Study of the Stimulus

Like it or not, the layout of the cards is not neutral. The objective characteristics of the 10 cards, including their figure-ground, shapes, colors, and shadings have been discussed in detail by Schachtel (1966) in terms of perceptual experience within a phenomenological framework. In France, Minkowska (1956), Muchielli (1968), and others have commented on the sensitivity and the affective climate of each card. Bohm (1955) tried, but not very convincingly, to assign an implicit symbolic meaning to each card. In the 1950s, some American researchers focused their attention on the so-called sexual and parental cards, using external criteria such as Osgood's semantic differential. Following Jung's ideas, one researcher proposed an original but poorly applicable interpretation of the stimuli. Much of the work of this kind has been detrimental to advances in Rorschach interpretation, because some psychologists, especially beginners, have taken these proposals literally without distinguishing between reality and fantasy.

This problem was reexamined from a different viewpoint by Bolzinger (1972), who utilized the technique of offering choices in the inquiry (i. e., asking subjects for their preferences among the cards) to confirm the implicit meaning of the cards. Taking into consideration the structural and sensory organization of the cards, the frequency of the associations given by subjects of various clinical and age groups, and also their own theoretical preferences, Rausch de Traubenberg and Boizou (1977) and Chabert (1983) developed a different approach to the underlying symbolic meaning of the blots. Their proposed hypotheses regarding the symbolic meaning of the cards stipulate that this meaning depends upon the level of the psychic functioning of the subject. One may suppose that beyond the perceptual configuration the subjects are going to give a "meaning" of another order depending on their affects, dreams, and fantasies, and in so doing "they personalize the reality." Experience with children's Rorschachs has shown that very young children and psychotic youngsters also may easily grasp the fantasy meaning of the stimuli and their potential symbolic references, especially those referring to the body and to relationships with parental images. As an example, a 4-year-old girl saw in Card IX "a beast that lives with its mother."

In protocols of adults some sensitivity to specific meanings of the cards is generally a very important clinical clue to psychological flexibility. The validity of this hypothesis in clinical practice is, in our opinion, highlighted by phenomenological and psychoanalytic theories.

15

An Illustrative Research Study

Recently we had the opportunity to examine the question of card speci-ficity in 73 protocols given by adolescents age 16 to 19 years attending senior high schools in Paris. This research was conducted by a team of psychologists under my direction in the Hospital of La Salpétriere in Paris and presented during the XIII International Congress of Ror-schach and Projective Techniques in Paris (Martin et al. 1991). Some of the most important results are summarized below. In this research per-cepts and contents were studied, for each card, in order to identify themes unique to adolescents, the significance of these themes, and their effects on judgment and adaptation.

To determine whether the cards have any specificity for non-patient adolescents, the research proceeded as follows. First, the frequencies of the formal features of the responses, the perceptual modes and determi-nants, were calculated from the 73 protocols taken as a whole. No statis-tically significant differences appeared between the boys and the girls in the sample, and the data of the whole group were therefore pooled. Next, we recorded for each card the formal characteristics of the re-sponses; the contents, classified according to the headings of an analyti-cal grid of "Affective Dynamics" (expression of drives, aggressivity, body image, sexual themes, narcissism, anxiety, depression, defense mecha-nisms) (Rausch de Traubenberg et al., 1990); and finally the themes of the responses, carefully examined to refine the data of the first protocol analysis.

These various kinds of analysis yielded the following results:

1. Whereas perceptual modes, determinants, and popular responses do not enable us to differentiate between boys and girls, they do allow us to divide the cards into four groups: (a) cards such as I and V, with maximal utilization of one location (W) and one determinant (F), which are more cognitive and social than emotional; (b) cards such as VIII, X, and above all VII and III, which trigger more flexible attitudes and more varied behaviors pertaining to social adaptation; (c) one ambivalent card (VI) in which perceptual modes are rather diversified (W% = 45%), whereas the form determinant is frequent and rigid, suggesting a strong socialization; and (d) two cards, II and IX, in which the location (W, D, Dd, S) is varied but reality testing (F+%) fails, af-fected by emotional reactions manifested through colors and move-ment responses.

2. Contents grouped according to the psychological dimensions of "Affective Dynamics" enabled us to differentiate to some extent the reactions of girls and boys. The most important observation in this regard is that the negative elements are mainly found on cards II and IX. Reality testing (F+%) is poor in concert with an apparent occasional disorganization of psychic functioning. This disorganization is reactivated by bodily and/or sexual concerns accompanied by a defensive mobilization more archaic here than on other cards.

3. The careful study of how verbalization (nouns, verbs, adjectives) unfolds and varies shows clear and obvious differences between girls and boys. These differences are not apparent when one considers only the psychometric data.

In summary, then, the distribution of *formal scores* through the 10 cards revealed two sensitive cards (II and IX), on which failure of control and loss of objective reality are likely to occur. The distribution of *contents* in terms of "Affective Dynamics" analysis confirms the sensitivity of these two cards and explains it in relation to the sensitivity to bodily integrity and to the archaic image of the mother; this analysis also identifies sexual differences with respect to expressions of aggressivity. A thematic analysis of the *discourse as a whole* emphasizes more clearly the concerns and the defense and coping mechanisms of each group.

By focusing the research on the stimulus itself, differential results were obtained that did not appear in a more traditional analysis. This emphasis is even more necessary when the Rorschach is used in extreme conditions such as with non-Western cultures and traumatic life-conditions. In these cases it would be inappropriate simply to apply the cues obtained in our clinical studies.

Other Approaches

A single mode of analysis can hardly account for the richness of the Rorschach, and for this reason numerous approaches from diverse viewpoints have been proposed. For my part I would merely like to emphasize the importance of themes related to body image and self representation.

Body Image

The use of the Rorschach in child psychology and child psychiatry research continuously confronts us with the importance of body image. Since originally proposed by Schilder (1973), this notion has been developed in various perspectives: phenomenological, personalistic, psychogenetic, and psychoanalytic. First empirically studied by Fisher and Cleveland (1958) and by Fisher (1970), this notion became a more scientific concept in Anzieu's work on the "skin ego" (1985) and in other work on the container/content relationship.

Within the limits of our research, we propose that *the Rorschach tests the presence of an integrated body image,* regardless of whether responses concerning the body are present or not. The starting point of this hypothesis is obviously the stimulus structure, constructed around a vertical median axis, well contrasted from the white background and outlined to mark off the inside from the outside. This stimulus, this perceptual pattern, this space is a bodily space, a "body," whether human, animal, botany, or inanimate object. The body can be simply named, described in terms suggesting great value ("a very beautiful butterfly," Card I), or presented as injured and mutilated ("a butterfly with ragged wings"; "a completely battered can," Card IV). In other words, the body is always cathected with libidinal energy and experienced in relation to the external world. Therefore, the body is not projected as a real or known entity or as an object of knowledge, but rather as an experienced entity that can be both subject and object of affects. *The bodily space becomes relational space.*

In children, these projections of body images are easy to find in both human and non-human percepts. Both types of responses reflect perceptual and conceptual differentiation, provided the percept is clearly defined without either overlapping or superpositions and provided well-defined homogeneous contents are given in a clearly stated determinant.

It is possible to look for the body images whether expressed in a direct or indirect manner, whether archaic or evolved in expression. Card I, for instance, is interpreted as "a spider which has swallowed a fly," a W contaminated response in which no image exists autonomously. By contrast, the response "it is a black fly" is more evolved because boundaries are not lost even though the form quality is not good. In young children various levels are often found in the same protocol, thus indicating some overlapping of perceptual modes. A study of the 10 cards (Boizou, Chabert, & Rausch de Traubenberg, 1978) as they are treated by children of various ages and personality structures led us to distinguish various lev-

18

els of individuation and differentiation and therefore various levels of self-representation and object relations.

In protocols of young schizophrenic adults, Chabert (1987) high-lighted "the links that join the body, the thought and their objects." In this case, the failure of cognitive processes goes hand-in-hand with damaged or fragmented body images. The body is no longer a unity, or a container, and consequently it cannot act as a basis for thinking. The links – body and thinking – are a theme particularly worth studying with projective techniques.

Self-Representation

The image of the projected body, from the most archaic to the most advanced level, is not a psychic agency. Loaded with diverse meanings, this image condenses the cathexis of the self and of the other and there-fore reflects the affective dimension of relationships with the surround-ing world. This affective attitude interacts with the perceptual and con-ceptual structure that it either mobilizes and organizes or deteriorates and disorganizes.

"Self-representation" is unconscious. It includes the body image as well as its surrounding relationships. These are interrelated; the body image creates the relationships which, in return, structure the body image itself. The concept of self-representation seems to account fully for these relations. It serves as a unifying principle, bringing together the various stages of qualitative and quantitative analysis in directing them towards the subject himself.

Myriam Orr had already, in 1958, begun to understand this notion of self-representation when she described the Rorschach contents as a psy-chic auto-portrait, the source of which would be the universal need of self-representation. More recently American authors, such as Mayman (1967) and Blatt (1976), developed methods for analyzing object repre-sentations. Mayman tried to grasp the affective and conceptual aspects of object representation. Blatt adopted a more cognitive approach in which clinical experience is considered from a developmental frame-work. Researchers such as Urist (1977), and more recently Ipp (1986) and others quoted by Lerner (1991), apply Mahler's theory of separa-tion-individuation and propose scales to assess the development of ob-ject relations.

The self-representation grid we proposed is not as ambitious (Rausch de Traubenberg & Sanglade, 1984). Its purpose is to establish the construct validity of the self-representation by multidisciplinary analysis of contents bringing to light subjects' fundamental stance vis á vis their body experience and object relations. To achieve this, we need to analyze all aspects of the body image itself – whether total or partial, its modes of interaction, action, and relation, its sexual differentiation, whether determined or not, and the degree to which it is differentiated or undifferentiated. This grid uses all contents, not only the human; this special score is given in addition to the traditional ones. As formulated at present the grid is a working tool aimed at objectifying and quantifying qualitative aspects, and it enables us to compare groups of subjects in comparison to the study of interferences between perceptual and fantasmatic activity, which is primarily useful in analyzing individual protocols.

Conclusion

This article presents some of my own and my colleagues' approaches to the Rorschach Test. They come from clinical practice, which itself has been influenced by teaching activities that, in turn, feed back to the clinical work. Teaching in which methodological issues, theoretical references, and clinical experience are intermingled deepens one's comprehension of the Rorschach. Teaching activities and clinical application to various groups of subjects renew the understanding of the projective data and therefore clarify their conceptual basis. Hence the Rorschach becomes *a tool for thinking* that can serve various psychological theories.

The test, an objective reality, allows numerous interpretations, cognitive, affective, and fantasmatic. These interpretations can be approached in very different ways depending upon one's goals and especially one's theoretical preferences. Yet neither the subject nor the psychologist enjoys complete freedom: The subject's creative freedom is restricted by the object stimulus, and the psychologist's interpretative freedom is limited by the testing situation itself, defined by a subject, an object, and a demand. The combinations of interactions among all these aspects seem to be infinite. It appears that everyone of us, whether a clinician, a researcher, or a teacher, has his or her characteristic viewpoint and approach; we focus on a particular pattern of combinations depending upon our attitude, our goals, and also our field of experience. This range of experience needs to be broadened in order to ensure an open-mindedness and a critical examination of one's own schemes, whether innate or acquired. Our contribution as "projective psychologists" is all the more valuable as we are able to add a creative dynamism to basic scientific knowledge.

The working instrument invented by H. Rorschach has proved to be as impressively rich as the man, Rorschach himself. He was a psychiatrist and a psychologist, a neurophysiologist, an artist, and an ethnologist, a man of science and a man of human contact, as modest as he was enthusiastic.

Résumé

L'hypothèse proposée ici est que dans le processus de la réponse face au Rorschach il y a une condensation d'interactions variées et mobiles entre le réel et l'imaginaire, l'activité perceptive et l'activité fantasmatique.

La proposition de Rorschach était que le test saisit l'intelligence et l'affectivité et c'est à partir de cette idée que j'ai élaboré le travail sur les interférences entre activité perceptive et activité fantasmatique.

Ces deux pôles se retrouvent aux différentes étapes de la passation et de l'interprétation du Rorschach. Il en est déjà ainsi dans la situation d'examen, les consignes données et le matériel stimulus, construit mais non fini, structuré mais ambigu, plein et creux. Les cotations des réponses expriment déjà ces deux aspects, à des degrés divers, mais c'est au niveau de l'interprétation des facteurs, interprétation dont la valeur n'est jamais univoque, que l'on saisit au mieux les interactions percept-fantasme, ces deux formes d'activité exprimant un besoin de personnalisation des conduites, une double expression de relation au monde externe et au monde interne.

C'es l'étude des Rorschach d'enfants qui a permis de comprendre, outre la place du corps, le rôle respectif de l'activité perceptive et fantasmatique et le rôle non seulement perturbateur mais parfois organisateur du fantasme. Les Rorschach de l'adulte montrent combien la simultanéité d'action de ces deux fonctions est garante d'un certain équilibre psychique. Ils indiquent également comment il peut y avoir déviance et pathologie par échec du perceptif ou par simple absence de l'imaginaire.

Un travail ponctuel récent attire l'attention sur le stimulus, le jeu des deux activités dans les significations symboliques possibles des dix planches du test pour des adolescents normaux. L'étude montre combien l'approche perceptive et cognitive est différente d'une planche à l'autre, et combien les contenus relatifs à des positions fantasmatiques archaïques, survenant à certaines planches, en désorganisent sporadiquement les modes perceptifs: les planches sensibles pour les adolescents sont II et IX.

Les thèmes "images du corps" et "représentation de soi" sont corrélatifs du thème central, "Rorschach, espace d'interactions". L'étude comparée de ces deux thèmes dans les tests d'enfants et d'adultes montre, entre autres, que les avatars dans les processus d'identification chez l'adulte renvoient aux difficultés des relations d'objet repérées chez l'enfant: ceci réfère implicitement à la psychopathologie sans qu'il soit possible d'établir une correspondance stricte entre ces troubles et les catégories nosographiques classiques.

Cet ensemble de propositions joint aux modes classiques d'analyse du Rorschach renouvelle l'étude du Rorschach et témoigne de l'extraordinaire richesse du test.

Resumen

El punto de vista de la autora consiste en que el proceso de respuesta incluye interacciones variadas entre los mundo real e imaginario, entre la actividad perceptiva y la actividad de fantasia.

La reflexión de la autora se basa en la sugerencia de H. Rorschach, según la cual el test evalúa inteligencia y afecto. De alli se deriva su concepto de interacciones entre actividad perceptiva y actividad de fantasia.

Referirse a este modelo de interacción parece relevante en cada etapa de la prueba, desde la administración hasta la interpretación: en la administración, con sus instrucciones particulares y material especifico, estructurado pero incompleto y ambiguo, lleno y vacio a un mismo tiempo; en las codificaciones también, en diversos grados; y, especialmente, en la interpretación de los factores, que no son nunca univocos. Las interacciones entre percepto y fantasme expresan la relación en ambos sentidos entre los mundos externo e interno.

El estudio del Rorschach en niños ha conducido a la autora a entender, tanto la importancia del cuerpo, como los roles respectivos de las actividades de percepción y de fantasia; las actividades de fantasia tienen, en los niños, tanto efectos organizadores como perturbadores. El Rorschach del adulto revela que la actividad simultánea de percepción y fantasia garantiza un balance psiquico; muestra también que ciertas conductas desviantes y manifestaciones patológicas pueden ser causadas por el fracaso de la actividad perceptiva, o la mera pérdida del mundo imaginario.

En un estudio reciente del Rorschach de adolescentes nopacientes, se prestó especial atención al estimulo y al interjuego de ambas actividades, ligado a los diferentes significados simbólicos de las diez láminas. Este estudio enfatiza la variedad de enfoques perceptivos y cognitivos, y cómo los modos perceptivos pueden ser temporalmente desorganizados por algunos contenidos referidos a fantasias arcaicas. Las láminas más sensibles para los adolescentes fueron la II y la IX.

Tópicos tales como "imagen corporal" y "representación de si mismo" se derivan del tema central "el Rorschach, espacio de interacciones". El estudio comparative de estos temas, en los Rorschach de niños y adultos, apunta a que las perturbaciones en los procesos de identificación del adulto remiten a dificultades del niño en la relación objetal. Ello establece un nexo implicito con la psicopatologia, pero sin fijar correspondencias estrictas entre estas perturbaciones y la nosologia clásica.

La proposición de la autora confluye con las formas clásicas de analizar el Rorschach y conduce a una renovación del estudio de la prueba. Da testimonio igualmente, acerca de la extraordinaria riqueza del test.

References

Anzieu, D. (1985) *Le Moi-Peau*. English translation *The Skin Ego*. 1989. Yale University Press.

Blatt, S. J., Brenneis, C., Schimek, J. G., & Glick, M. (1976). *A developmental analysis of the concept of the object on the Rorschach*. Unpublished manual.

Blatt, S. J., & Ritzler, B. A. (1974). Thought disorder and boundary disturbances in psychosis. *Journal of Consulting and Clinical Psychology*, *42*, 370–381.

Bohm, E. (1955). *Traité du Psychodiagnostic de Rorschach*, tr. fr. Paris, Presses Universitaires de France (épuisé), nouvelle traduction par H. Hernert, Paris, Masson, 1985.

Boizou, M. F., Chabert, C., & Rausch de Traubenberg, N. (1978). Représentation de soi. Identité, identification au Rorschach chez l'enfant et l'adulte. *Bulletin de Psychologie*, *339*, XXXII, 271–277.

Bolzinger, A. (1972). Pour un diagnostic des structures latentes du test de Rorschach. *Bulletin de Psychologie, 305*, XXVI, (10–11) 5171–581.

Bower, P. A., Testin, R., & Roberts, A. (1960). Rorschach diagnosis by systematic combining of content, thought process and determinant scales. *Genetic Psychology Monographs, 62*, 105–183.

Chabert, C. (1983). *Le Rorschach en clinique adulte. Interprétation psychanalytique.* Paris: Dunod.

Chabert, C. (1987). *La psychopathologie a l'épreuve du Rorschach*, Paris: Dunod.

Cosnier, J. (1969). Psycholinguistique et technique projective. *Bulletin de la Société Francaise du Rorschach et des Méthodes Projective, 23*, 5–13.

Dworetzki, G. (1939). *Le test de Rorschach et l'évolution de la perception.* Genéve: Naville.

Engel, M. (1963). On the psychological testing of borderline children. *Archives of General Psychiatry, 8*, 426–434.

Fairbarn, W. (1952). *An object relations theory of the personality.* New York: Basic Books.

Fisher, S., & Cleveland, S. E. (1958). *Body image and personality.* Princeton, New Jersey: D. Van Nostrand Co.

Fisher, S. (1970). *Body experience in fantasy and behavior.* New York – Appleton-Century-Crofts.

Friedman, H. (1953). Perceptual regression in schizophrenia, an hypothesis suggested by the use of the Rorschach Test. *Journal of Projective Techniques, 17*, 171–185.

Hemmendinger, L. (1960). Developmental theory and the Rorschach method. In M. A. Rickers-Ovsiankina (Ed.), *Rorschach psychology* (pp. 58–79). New York: Wiley.

Ipp (1986). *Object relations of feminine boys: a Rorschach assessment.* Unpublished doctoral dissertation, York University.

Lagache, D. (1957). La rêverie imageante, conduite adaptative au test de Rorschach. *Bulletin du Groupement francais du Rorschach, 9*, 3–11.

Lerner, P. M. (1991). *Psychoanalytic theory and the Rorschach.* Hillsdale, NY: Analytic Press.

Lerner, P., & Lerner, H. (1980). Rorschach assessment of primitive defenses in borderline personality structure. In J. Kwawer, H. Lerner, P. Lerner, & A. Sugarman (Eds.), *Borderline phenomena and the Rorschach test* (pp. 257–274). New York: International Universities Press.

Mahler, M., Pine, F., & Bergman, A. (1975). *The psychological birth of the human infant.* New York: Basic Books.

Martin, M., Bloche-Lainé, F., Duplant, N., Poggionovo, M. P., & Rausch de Traubenberg, N. (1991). Expression actuelle au Rorschach du fonctionnement psychique d'adolescents normalement scolarisés. *Rorschachiana XVII.* Paris-Berne: ECPA – Hans Huber, pp. 313–318.

Mayman, M. (1967). Object representations and object relationships in Rorschach responses. *Journal of Projective Techniques and Personality Assessment, 31*, 17–24.

Mayman, M. (1970). Reality contact, defense effectiveness and psychopathology in Rorschach form-level scores. In B. Klopfer, M. Meyer, & F. Brawer (Eds.), *Develop-*

ments in Rorschach Technique (Vol. III, pp. 11–44). New York: Harcourt, Brace Jovanovitch.

Minkowska, F. (1956). *Le Rorschach. A la recherche du monde des formes.* Paris: Desclée de Brouwer.

Mucchielli, R. (1968). *La dynamique du Rorschach.* Paris: Presses Universitaires de France.

Orr, M. (1958). Le test de Rorschach et l'imago maternelle. Monograhie du *Bulletin du Groupement Francais du Rorschach.*

Piaget, J. (1937). *The construction of reality in the child.* New York: Basic Books, 1954.

Rausch de Traubenberg, N., Boizou, M. F., Bloche-Lainé, F., Chabert, C. Des Ligneris, J., & Ponroy, R. (1973). Organisation prépsychotique et psychotique de la personnalité chez l'enfant a travers les techniques projective. *Psychologie Francaise, 18*, 213–231.

Rausch de Traubenberg, N., & Boizou, M. F. (1980). Pre-psychotic conditions in children as manifested in their perception of fantasy experience on Rorschach and thematic tests. In J. Kwawer, H. Lerner, P. Lerner, A. Sugarman (Eds.), *Borderline phenomena and the Rorschach test* (pp. 395–409). New York: International Universities Press.

Rausch de Traubenberg (1985). Le Rorschach, espace d'interactions. *Bulletin de Psychologie,* "Psychologie Projective III," 376, XXXIV, (11–15), 659–661.

Rausch de Traubenberg, N., & Sanglade, A. (1984). Représentation de soi et relation d'objet au Rorschach. Grille de représentation de soi. *Revue de Psychologie Appliquée, 34*, 1, 41–57.

Rausch de Traubenberg, N., Bloche-Lainé, F., Boizou, M. F., Duplant, N., Martin, M., & Poggionovo, M. P. (1990). Modalités d'analyse de la dynamique affective au Rorschach. *Revue de Psychologie Appliquée, 40*, 245–258.

Rorschach, H. (1921). *Psychodiagnostic,* tr. fr. Paris: Presses Universitaires de France, 1947.

Schachtel, E. (1966). *Experiential foundations of Rorschach's Test.* New York: Basic Books.

Schafer, R. (1954). *Psychoanalytic interpretation in Rorschach testing.* New York: Grune & Stratton.

Schilder, P. (1973). *L'image du corps.* Paris: Gallimard.

Urist, G. (1977). The Rorschach test and the assessment of object relations. *Journal of Personality Assessment, 41*, 3–9.

Werner, H. (1940). *Comparative psychology of mental development.* New York: International Universities Press.

Winnicott, D. W. (1975). *Jeu et réalité, l'espace potentiel.* Paris: Gallimard.

Zulliger, H. (1949). Der statische, der dynamische und der tiefenpsychologische Befund bei der Interpretation des Formdeutversuch, *Psyche.*

The Present Status of the Rorschach Test in Spain

Pilar Ortiz Quintana

Complutense University of Madrid, Spain

Vera Campo

Catalan Society of Rorschach, Spain

This paper addresses the present status of the Rorschach Test in Spain. Information has been gathered concerning its teaching in the university, both at the degree level and in post-graduate studies, and allow with respect to research work with the test. We would also have liked to comment on its use in clinical practice, but sufficiently representative data were not available to us. Our report concerns the period between 1984 and 1991, dating from the XI International Congress of Rorschach and Projective Techniques held in Barcelona.

The first work on the Rorschach Test in Spain was published by Dr. Sacristán in 1925 and was intended to promote the new method. The research with the Rorschach technique began in 1932. The most important publication during these early years was "The Psychodiagnosis of Rorschach" by Dr. Salas (1944), which was based on a very large sample of 2,138 protocols of non-patients of various ages and 1,148 patient protocols. Given the importance of this work, it became an obligatory reference work in Spain for many years.

During the subsequent decades frequent publications appeared that promoted the gradual incorporation of the Rorschach Test into the work of Spanish psychologists and psychiatrists. Agustín Serrate was one of the great driving forces behind this development, on the basis of his translation of the work of Bohm and his initiation of contacts with Rorschach workers in other countries. His scientific presence at the International Congresses of Rorschach and Projective Techniques led to his being entrusted with the organization of the VIII International Congress in Zaragoza in 1971. This Congress resulted in the creation of the Sociedad Española del Rorschach y Métodos Proyectivos (SERYMP) one year later.

Sociedad Espanola del Rorschach y Metodos Proyectivos

Since its creation until now, the Sociedad Espanola del Rorschach y Metodos Proyectivos (SERYMP) has provided the main meeting point for Spanish clinicians and researchers in projective methods. Its aims are the promotion and development of these techniques, both in clinical and research applications, attention to their scientific value, and the establishment of collaboration with other similar societies at home and abroad.

Membership in SERYMP requires a degree or diploma in Psychology or a degree in Medicine in the specialty of Psychiatry; a minimum of 2 years of professional experience; and research work (whether published or not) on the Rorschach or some other projective technique.

With regard to research, the aim of the Society is to act as a registration center for research projects in projective psychology, for which purpose it carries out a variety of activities: training courses, scientific meetings, and since 1988, the publication of the *Revista de la Sociedad Española del Rorschach y Métodos Proyectivos*. The journal has published articles on the use and development of projective techniques in clinical and research work, together with transcultural studies and bibliographic information. Translations have also been made of significant articles from foreign publications.

Teaching

In Spain, as in many other countries, psychodiagnosis has been receding into a place of secondary importance in the role of psychologists. Traditional techniques are encountering serious challenge, especially from behavioral perspectives, which have shown increasing growth in our universities. In conjunction with a loss of status for traditional clinical methods, the teaching of projective techniques has been losing ground in our degree studies.

By way of example we can take two of our universities that, by virtue of having the largest number of students and the strongest tradition, could be considered representative of the academic situation in our country: the Complutense University of Madrid and the Central University of Barcelona.

In the Complutense University of Madrid degree studies in Psychology began in 1969. Until 1977 there was only one course in psychodiagnosis in which projective techniques were included. The program of studies established in 1977 included three courses: Psychometric Tests, Projective Tests, and Psychodiagnosis. The course on Projective Tests was 1 year in length and obligatory for all students. The program of studies as revised in 1984 included Psychological Assessment I, which was required of all degree students, and Psychological Assessment II and Psychodiagnosis, which were required only for students specializing specializing in Clinical Psychology. Since then and up to the present time, projective techniques constitute only one part of the course Psychological Assessment II.

In the Central University of Barcelona, there has been since the beginning of the program of psychological studies in 1971 just an optional course in projective techniques. For the past 3 years students have had the option of choosing between a general course or a course specifically devoted to the Rorschach Test.

At present, with the incorporation into the European Economic Community, all university programs of study in Spain are being reorganized. Next year, new programs will become operational in which projective techniques will disappear from all of the colleges which they remain at present. These new programs of study include obligatory courses for all Faculties of Psychology, among which is Psychological Assessment. Each Faculty organizes its own curriculum, which usually includes one other course in psychodiagnosis. Analysis of the descriptions of these new courses reveals that projective techniques play a very small role in them – although, among projective techniques, the Rorschach remains the most readily accepted.

Among university teachers of clinical psychology there are a great many experts in the Rorschach Test who explain it as thoroughly as possible within the confines of very restrictive programs. But let us not deceive ourselves: in the academic field other methods of psychological assessment – not so much of psychodignosis – are receiving ever greater acceptance.

In spite of all this, there continues to be a high demand for postgraduate courses in the Rorschach. Some doctoral programs in clinical psychology include courses devoted to the Rorschach Test, and this is also the case in some master's level programs given in the university.

Outside of the academic field the most important work on the Rorschach has been undertaken by the Sociedad Catalana del Rorschach y Métodos Proyectivos, which is a member of SERYMP. Since its founding in 1975, it has offered Rorschach courses at three levels of advancement, each 9 months in duration with 1–1/2 hours per week of instruction. At present, the Catalan Society also teaches a 1-year course on "Rorschach in Personnel Selection," a 6-month course on "Rorschach in Forensic Psychology," and additional courses of "Rorschach for Children" and "Rorschach in Adolescence."

For several years a branch of Exner's "Rorschach Workshops" has operated in Madrid, offering courses at three levels with a duration of one school year and meeting 1-1/2 hours per week. In addition to these various courses, many instructional opportunities are offered to individuals on a private basis.

Both in the courses of the Sociedad Catalana, in the "Rorschach Workshops" in Madrid, and in the majority of the private instruction, teaching is based on Exner's Comprehensive System. The Comprehensive System is the most firmly established Rorschach method in Spain and the most widely accepted academically. Some private courses still teach the system of Bohm, which for many years had been the most widely accepted system. No other Rorschach systems have had much acceptance in Spain.

Research

Presentations

The Spanish contribution to International Congresses of Rorschach and Projective Methods has been rather limited. At the XI Congress, held in Barcelona in 1984, a total of 138 papers were presented, of which 14 were Spanish (10% of the total); of these, eight were concerned with Rorschach (57% of the Spanish contribution).

At the XII Congress, held in Brazil in 1987, of a total of 175 contributions, 14 were Spanish, (8% of the total); of these, 12 dealt with the Rorschach (85% of the Spanish total).

At the XIII Congress, held in Paris in 1990, production increased notably at the international level. There were 336 presentations, 31 of them

Spanish (9% of the total); of these, 23 concerned the Rorschach Test (74% of the Spanish material). It can thus be seen that the interest of Spanish researchers and clinicians in projective methods in general and the Rorschach Test in particular has been increasing.

At the national level, of the many congresses that are held in the field of psychology, we shall refer only to those that most specifically embrace the area of psychodiagnosis: Sociedad Española del Rorschach y Métodos Proyectivos (1986, 1989, 1991), Evaluación Psicológica (1984, 1987, 1990), and Colegio Oficial de Psicólogos (1984, 1990). At the 3rd Congreso de Evaluación Psicológica (1990), a symposium was organized on "Contributions of the Rorschach to Psychological Assessment." At the 2nd Congreso del Colegio Oficial de Psicólogos (1990), another symposium was organized on "Perspectives in Research on Projective Techniques."

The total number of contributions on Rorschach at the above-mentioned national congresses was 62, of which 41 (66%) were presented at the Congresses of the Sociedad del Rorschach y Métodos Proyectivos.

Taken together, the contributions to international and national congresses total 105 pieces of work on the Rorschach. Table 1 shows the frequency with which various topics were addressed in these presentations.

Table 1. Frequency of topics in congress presentations.

Topic	International	National	Total	% Total
Technical aspects	13	11	24	22.8
Schizophrenia & psychosis	5	10	15	14.3
Children	3	10	13	12.3
Psychosomatic and physical disorders	3	8	11	10.4
Antisocial disorders (drugs, alcohol, delinquency)	6	4	10	9.6
Depression	2	5	7	6.7
Borderline and narcissistic	2	5	7	6.7
Treatment assessment	3	4	7	6.7
Personnel selection	2	3	5	4.8
Perversion	2	2	4	3.8
Old age	0	2	2	1.9

Publications

During the period since 1984 six books dealing with the Rorschach have been published in Spain. Campo (1988a) investigates the implications of using the Rorschach with children, its relationship to the clinical history and to other diagnostic instruments, its usefulness in prognosis, and its application in follow-up and treatment assessment. Campo also employs a theoretical-clinical perspective to explore the interpretive significance of various components of the test. Finally, she reviews Rorschach features in some psychopathological disorders. Campo's approach is basically descriptive and dynamic. She integrates Exner's Comprehensive System with a psychoanalytic approach in order to achieve a broad view of personality through Rorschach. Campo also published a chapter on high M frequency in children under age 10 (1988b) in which she suggests that this apparent pseudo- maturity is usually a negative prognostic indicator related to an early premature structuring of character.

The work of Vives (1989) revolves around two themes that constitute her primary interest: psychodiagnosis with the Rorschach and schizophrenia. Vives first reviews schizophrenia historically from Freudian, genetic, and cognitive perspectives. She then provides a classification of thought disorders according to the Research Diagnostic Criteria and relates these variables to diagnostic indices in the Rorschach. By comparing data from samples of 30 acute and 30 chronic schizophrenics with Exner's normative data for non- patients and inpatients, Vives establishes highly consistent identifying variables and structural prognostic indices for schizophrenia.

A book by Jiménez (1990) is written primarily from a central Central European perspective, although the contributions of American Rorschachers are not ignored. This volume is basically a reference source on essential concepts and different problems encountered by the beginner. It is written in standard casebook fashion: presentation of background information, administration of the test, sequence of scores, psychogram, and diagnosis. In the last part of the book a study on the "Láminas Proyectivas" by Rodrigues Isidoro is mentioned and some data from it are presented.

Jiménez and Diego (1991a) review work on the "Láminas Proyectivas," the first studies on which were presented at the XI International Congress in Barcelona (1984). They summarize various research findings that support the joint use of the Rorschach and the "Láminas Proyectivas" in differential diagnosis.

31

Portuondo (1989) provides an overview of his previous publications on the Rorschach. In the first part of his book he discusses scoring, and in the second part he discusses the psychoanalytic approach to Rorschach and expands on such topics as as "life and death," "originality," and "Eros and Thanatos" and their analysis by means of the Rorschach.

In addition to these books on the Rorschach, some chapters on Rorschach have been published in other books used as supplementary texts for university students. Ortiz (1990a, 1990b) has carried out an up-to-date review with regard to administration, evaluation, and interpretation according to Exner's Comprehensive System, and Avila and Rodriguez (1990) have written a general introduction in which they present a historical review of the principal Rorschach systems, the basic lines of research with the Rorschach, and methodological considerations in working with the test.

Turning to publications in journals, a bibliographic search using available data bases on Spanish publications revealed 66 articles on the Rorschach test during the 1984- 1991 period. The frequency of the most common topics in these journal articles is shown in Table 2. As can be seen, the topic frequency in these publications follows a trend similar to that of the contributions presented at congresses.

Table 2. Frequency of topics in journal articles.

Topic	Number	%
Technical aspects	13	20
Schizophrenia and psychosis	12	18.2
Psychosomatic and physical disorders	10	15.1
Children	9	13.6
Antisocial disorders (drugs, alcohol, delinquency)	5	7.6
Borderline and narcissistic	3	4.5
Treatment assessment	3	4.5
Old age	3	4.5
Depression	2	3.0
Perversion	2	3.0
Personnel selection	2	3.0
Other	2	3.0

Studies on *technical aspects* of the Rorschach have been most frequent. A bibliometric study by Márquez (1986) pulls together ample informa-

tion concerning the use of the Rorschach and trends in Rorschach research at the international level for the period 1975–1982, but does not
cover Spanish publications. The same is true of a review carried out by
Rodriguez (1990) of trends in Rorschach teaching, practice, and research and of the scientific status of the instrument.

Among works that refer specifically to Spanish people, a study by Larraz and Valero (1988) of Popular responses on the Rorschach Test
among residents of Barcelona stands out in importance. Also important
are studies by Sendín (1987b, 1988) that present normative data on a
very broad sample and that show the results of an intergroup factorial
analysis involving patient and nonpatient subjects (Sendin, 1990a,
1990b).

In other significant work, the response process to the Rorschach stimuli from the point of view of information processing has been studied
by Márquez et al. (1985) and by Márquez and Fernández Ballesteros
(1988). The subject of interpretation has been dealt with in a general
manner by Campo et al.(1987) and more specifically with respect to the
evaluation and interpretation of texture by Campo (1991a). Finally, Ros
(1989) has underlined the importance of the interpretation of symbols
in the Rorschach and the reliability of the test in forensic applications
(1991).

Second in frequency have been studies on *schizophrenia and pscychosis*.
Some of these studies focus on the discriminative ability of the Rorschach in acute schizophrenia, taking the Research Diagnostic Criteria
as criterion (Vives, 1985a, 1985b, 1986, 1991). Vizcarro (1986) examines
the validity of Exner's System with Spanish schizophrenic subjects. Piotrowski's guidelines are followed in two studies of signs of organicity,
one involving subjects with residual schizophrenia (Salamero et al. 1990)
and the other concerned with epileptic psychosis (Blanco et al. 1986).
Ruiz et al. (1987, 1989) report a search for diagnostic indices paranoid
schizophrenia, and Martínez and Navarro (1985) present a case analysis
of a patient with schizoaffective schizophrenia.

Next in frequency, studies on *psychosomatic and physical disorders*, are of
interest to Spanish researchers but involve a wide diversity of topics. The
most common among these are psychological functioning in obese subjects (Galan, 1988) and anorexics (Campos, 1988; Velilla et al., 1984);
emotional and alexithymic indicators in psychosomatic adolescents
(Diaz Curie), 1998); and the study of a case of alopecia (Rodriguez Linde
& Herrero, 1986). Also of significance are studies of the impact of para-
plegia on body image and self concept, based on Exner's Self Percpetion

Cluster, by Ortiz (1990c, 1991); of the characteristics of psychological functioning attibutable to the experience of voluntary abortion by Tuset (1990); and of personality traits in coronary patients by Rus (1986).

Proceeding down the list, the studies with *children* also involve a range of topics. The most studied topic is cognitive functioning, as illustrated by research on the relationships between Field Dependence-Independence and the Rorschach (Forns et al., 1985); on differential cognitive style (Reflexiveness-Impulsiveness) inferred from Rorschach profiles (Quiroga, 1888b); and on relationships between Field Dependence-Independence and life style (Rodríguez Sutil, 1984). Other developmental research of note includes two studies of characteristics in hyperactive children (León & Valencia, 1986; Valencia & León, 1987); a comparative study of enuretic and nonenuretic children (Hierro, 1986); an investigation of learning difficulties and developmental prognosis (Campo, 1991b); and an analysis of body image and body experience in children with learning difficulties (Megías & Más, 1986).

Research on *antisocial disorders* has centered on delineating the personality characteristics of persons showing problem behavior. Two studies deal with delinquents in prison (Belín, 1985; Jiménez & Diego, 1991b). One concerns alcoholics (Vázquez & Benavente, 1987), and two others examine heroin addicts (Vargas et al., 1984, 1985).

With regard to *borderline and narcissistic* disorders, the basic aspects of the borderline personality are studied by Campo and Vilar (1990a, 1990b), with particular attention to the analysis of symbiotic contents, defenses, and object relations. The narcissistic personality is examined with particular attention to reflection and vista responses by Campo et al. (1991).

Treatment assessment is dealt with in three publications: Rorschach as a method of treatment assessment (Sendín & García, 1987); follow-up of the long-term course of a treatment case by means of the Rorschach and the Object Relations Test (Campo et al., 1988); and assessment of the efficacy of psychodrama as a therapeutic method in schizophrenia (Alvarez, 1987).

Studies on *old age* examine the organic deterioration produced by senile dementia as assessed with Piotrowski's indices (Insúa & Loza, 1988) and differential personality characteristics among the elderly (Rubio, 1985; Valsuárez, 1984).

Psychosexual disorders and the mental organization of subjects with *perversion* analyzed by Pérez et al. (1991), and a case of feminine transsexualism is presented by Jiménez and Pérez (1984).

The two articles on *depression* (Blanco et al., 1985; Ruiz, 1986) describe efforts to differentiate between endogenous depression and neurotic depression by means of Rorschach indices.

In the field of *personnel selection*, Mateo (1988) shows relationships between personality traits and leadership potential, and Ros (1988) compares two groups that have in common an employment position involving authority or substantial responsibility.

As a final note on these 66 published articles, the scoring systems used in them were as follows: Exner's Comprehensive System – 35; Bohm's Method – 7; Piotrowski's Method – 2; Klopfer's Method – 1; not specified – 19; theoretical – 2.

Doctoral Theses

A total 15 doctoral theses concerning the Rorschach were completed in Spain during the 1984–1991 period, and the data base may not be complete in this regard. All 15 are listed in the bibliography. The theses of Campo (1986) and Vives (1988) have already been mentioned in the section on publications. Some of the others are summarized briefly in this section.

Sendín (1989) investigated the factorial structure of the Rorschach with a sample of 359 subjects comprising four groups: non-patients, inpatient schizophrenics, inpatient non- schizophrenics, and ambulatory patients. Her normative data for the Spanish population and her factorial analyses are likely to find many useful theoretical and practical applications.

Jiménez (1987) carried out a study of schizophrenic deterioration through a structural analysis of language as used in formulation TAT responses. The Rorschach was among other techniques utilized to objectify criteria of deterioration.

The vulnerability of the Rorschach Test and of the MMPI to simulation of depression was studied by Ros (1990), who collected data from 16 patients, 8 nonpatient controls, and 16 simulators who were given some pretest information about depression. The Rorschach variables used were Exner's Depression Index (DEPI) and Coping Deficit Index (CDI). The MMPI variables were Scales 2, 7, and 8. The results showed that subjects of normal intelligence, when motivated and provided with information on the disorder, can simulate the DEPI index, but not the CDI. Combined use of both variables nevertheless prevented false positives among the simulators. On the MMPI the simulator group did not obtain elevated scores on Scales 2, 7, and 8.

Tuset (1990) studied the personality of 50 patients who had suffered heart attacks. These patients were tested during their hospitalization and again 3 months later to discriminate between reactions to the trauma of their illness and their more stable personality characteristics. Their relatively stable characteristics were low productivity, restricted and impulsive affective response, denial of the existence of internal or external demands, few adaptative resources, little interest in interpersonal relations, and an excessively idiographic perception of reality.

Ortiz (1990c) studied self-concept in 50 male paraplegics as measured by Exner's Self Perception Cluster and TSCS. Comparison with data from a control group of 50 male non- paraplegics revealed significant differences between the two groups. The paraplegics showed a more negative self concept, more concern about their body being vulnerable to harm, more dependency, more difficulties in interpersonal relationships, greater social isolation, and more introspection.

Hierro (1984) sought to find some common personality dynamics in enuretic children. She compared 42 enuretic children with 43 non-enuretic children, and she found that the enuretic children were more likely to show poor contact with reality, little affective stimulation, more painful experiences, low self-esteem, few adaptative resources, and impoverished interpersonal relations.

Quiroga (1988a), in a study of cognitive styles, carried out an exhaustive bibliographic review on Field Dependence- Independence. In her empirical work she examined cognitive and non-cognitive differential characteristics associated with Field Dependence-Independence in 96 subjects age 8 to 14 years, using an analysis of Rorschach profiles according to different cognitive style groups.

Aquirre (1990) carried out an observation of characteristics of the process of identification, as conceptualized psychoanalytically, in two groups of 38 and 40 adolescents. An analysis of group and individual characteristics revealed that subjects chosen as models of identification behave homogeneously with respect to values, whereas subjects rejected as models show opposite values.

Rovira (1990) profiled the internal structure of the non- aggressive delinquent subject (DSM-III) with a view to prevention and treatment. He used a sample of 43 female adolescents age 13 to 16 years being held in an Observation Center for having committed certain offenses and a control group of 43 non-offending students of the same age. The offender group was lower in socioeconomic class and differed from the control group in aspects of perception and thought that suggest cognitive immaturity as distinctive of this offender group.

Diego (1989) compared the Rorschach protocols of 105 adult criminals with those of 111 soldiers. Using a variety of psychometric and other projective techniques as well, he concluded that the projective techniques were more discriminative than the psychometric ones. Diego was also able to identify a Rorschach constellation with high concurrent validity for the presence of antisocial disorder.

Ruiz (1984), with a sample of 107 juvenile delinquents who were given the WISC and the Rorschach, established a series of differentiating variables for two clearly defined groups: occasional and habitual delinquents. She also developed a typology of juvenile delinquency.

Conclusions

Having reviewed the present status of the Rorschach Test in Spain, we see it as promising. It is encouraging to verify that interest in this technique has not diminished in spite of the fact that the new curriculum for degree courses in psychology has meant a reduction in the number of hours allotted to the teaching of the test. On checking the number of publications on a biennial basis, we find that there were 19 between 1984 and 1985; 15 between 1986 and 1987; 20 between 1988 and 1989; and 22 between 1990 and 1991, the highest number corresponding to the years following the International Congresses.

We note the lack of information on the scoring system used in many of the papers reviewed. It does tend to be indicated in those that use Exner's Comprehensive System, and in some it can be deduced from the nomenclature or terminology. Samples are usually sufficiently large, although they are not always well defined. The designs, in general, reach a high level of methodological rigor. The topics investigated are many, and interest is centered on clinical and methodological aspects.

Given the importance being acquired by the Rorschach Test, it is becoming increasingly necessary to have access to sufficiently abundant normative data on the Spanish population. We know that this work is being carried out and hope that it will soon be available.

Résumé

Cet article évalue le statut actuel du test de Rorschach en Espagne, du point de vue de l'enseignement et de la recherche. L'article débute avec un bref historique de la Société Espagnole du Rorschach et des Méthodes Projectives. Ensuite, les événements marquants des années 1984 à 1991 sont examinés, période qui correspond à l'intervalle écoulé entre le XIème et le XIIIème Congrès International de Rorschach.

Du point de vue de l'enseignement du Rorschach, une description en est donnée pour les niveaux de licence et les niveaux postgradués. Au niveau de la licence, il semblerait que loin d'être largement acceptés, les cours relatifs aux techniques projectives perdent du terrain dans les programmes d'études les plus récents. En dépit de cet état de fait, une demande considérable de cours postgradués sur le Rorschach continue d'exister.

L'analyse des recherches se centre sur les présentations, les rencontres nationales et internationales, les publications et les thèses de doctorat. Le nombre total de présentations s'élève à 105, dont 62 communications présentées à des rencontres nationales et 43 à des rencontres internationales. Le nombre de publications sur le Rorschach, pendant cette période, compte six livres et 66 articles de revues. La majorité d'entre eux concerne des questions de technique, suivi – d'après la fréquence – par des études sur la schizophrénie et la psychose, les troubles psychosomatiques et physiques, l'utilisation du Rorschach avec des enfants et les troubles antisociaux. 15 thèses de doctorat furent complétées et sont brièvement résumées dans l'article. Le système de cotation le plus fréquemment utilisé est le Système Synthétique d'Exner, quoique dans de nombreux articles, aucun système de cotation ne soit spécifié.

Enfin, bien que les changements dans les programmes d'études de licence en psychologie aient entraîné un enseignement réduit du Rorschach dans les universités, l'intérêt pour cette technique continue de croître. Cette croissance se reflète à la fois dans l'augmentation du nombre de recherches et dans l'amélioration de leur qualité scientifique.

Resumen

En este articulo se analiza la situación actual del Test de Rorschach en España en las áreas de enseñanza e investigación. Previamente, se lleva a cabo un breve recorrido histórico y una reseña sobre la Sociedad Española del Rorschach y Métodos Proyectivos.

El estudio enmarca el periodo 1984-1991, correspondiente al intervalo entre el XI y XIII Congresos Internacionales del Rorschach y Técnicas Proyectivas.

En cuanto a la enseñanza, se lleva a cabo un revisión de la docencia en los niveles de licenciatura y de postgrado. A nivel de estudios de licenciatura, se puede constatar cómo siendo el Test de Rorschach la técnica más acreditada, el conjunto de contenidos sobre Técnicas Poyectivas ha ido perdiendo espacio en los últimos Planes de Estudios, aunque el Test de Rorschach es la más acreditada. A pesar de todo, sigue habiendo una alta demanda de cursos de postgrado en Rorschach.

El análisis de la investigación se centra en: Comunicaciones a Congresos Nacionales e Internacionales, Publicaciones y Tesis Doctorales. El total de trabajos preséntados a congresos es de 105, de los cuales 62 corresponden a Congresos Nacionales y 43 a Congresos Internacionales. En cuanto a las publicaciones, hemos constatado la publicación de 6 libros y 66 articulos. La variedad de temas investigados es amplia, el mayor número de trabajos se centra en estudios sobre la técnica, seguidos de los estudios sobre esquizofrenia y psicosis, trastornos psicosomáticos y fisicos, Rorschach con niños, etc. En cuanto a las Tesis Doctorales, se han presentado 15 Tesis Doctorales, de las que se expone un breve resumen.

Respecto al sistema de valoración utilizado, el Sistema Comprensivo de Exner ocupa el primer lugar, aunque en muchos de los trabajos revisados no queda especificado.

De esta revisión podemos concluir que, a pesar de haber disminuido la enseñanza del Rorschach en los estudios universitarios, el interés por esta técnica va en aumento tanto por el número de investigaciones realizadas como por su calidad cientifica.

References

Aguirre, G. (1990). Adolescencia y procesos de identificación. Tesis Doctoral. Universidad Central de Barcelona.

Alvarez, P. (1987). Psicodrama y esquizofrenia crónica. Un estudio clínico y sociométrico. *Revista de la Asociación Española de Neuropsiquiatría*, 8(24), 53–84.

Apodaka, P., & Redondo, R. (1985). Implicaciones aptitudinales de la introtensión y de la ausencia de respuestas de movimiento humano en el Test de Rorschach. *Psiquis*, 6(6), 73–78.

Apodaka, P., & Martinez, M.C. (1985). El Test de Rorschach en la medida de las aptitudes. *Cuadernos de Psicología*, 9/1, 2 época, 111–125.

Avila, A., & Rodriguez, C. (1989). Introducción al estudio del Rorschach y sus derivados. En AVILA, A. (Ed.) *Evaluación Psicológica II*. Universidad Complutense de Madrid.

Ballesteros, P., & Quiroga, M.A. (1984). Estudio comparativo a través de los perfiles del Rorschach en niños. *I Congreso del Colegio Oficial de Psicólogos, Area* 3, 263–266.

Blanco, A. et al.(1986). Utilidad de las pruebas psicológicas para la detección del deterioro psicoorgánico en las psicosis epilépticas. *Revista del Departamento de Psiquiatría de la Facultad de Medicina de Barcelona*, 13(1), 1–19.

Blanco, A. et al. (1985). La utilidad de las pruebas proyectivas en la discriminación de las formas de depresión. *Phronesis*, 5, 297–304.

Campo, V. (1986). Los niños y el Rorschach. Aspectos clínicos, investigación y aplicación. Tesis Doctoral. Universidad Central de Barcelona.

Campo, V. (1988a). *Los niños y el Rorschach. Aspectos clínicos, investigación y aplicación.* Valencia. Promolibro.

Campo, V. (1988b). Some thoughts on M in relation to the early structuring of character in children. In Lerner, P.M. & LERNER, H.D. (Eds.) *Primitive mental states and the Rorschach.* Connecticut. International Universities Press.

Campo, V. (1991a). Learning difficulties and the Rorschach. *Rorschachiana*, XVII, 340–342.

Campo, V. (1991b). On Texture: Scoring and Interpretation. *British Journal of Projective Psychology.* 36(2).

Campo, V., Dow, N., & Tuset, A. (1988). Rorschach, ORT and follow-up. *British Journal of Projective Psychology.* 33(2), 31–53.

Campo, V., Galan, F., & Rovira, F. (1991). Consideraciones acerca del narcisismo: Estudio de un grupo de sujetos con respuestas de reflejo en el Rorschach. *Revista de la Sociedad Española del Rorschach y Métodos Proyectivos.* 4,33–38.

Campo, V., & Vilar, N. (1990a). Contenidos simbióticos y el trastorno límite de la personalidad. *II Congreso del Colegio Oficial de Psicólogos.* 7, 317–324.

Campo, V., & Vilar, N. (1990b). Acerca de los contenidos, defensas y relaciones objetales borderline. *Revista de la Sociedad Española del Rorschach y Métodos Proyectivos.* 3, 28–32.

Campo, V., Vilar, N., & Jacherasky, L. (1987). Reflexiones en torno a la interpretación en Rorschach. *Rorschachiana.* XVI.

Campos, S. (1988). Caso clínico. Un caso de anorexia nervosa. *Folia Neuropsiquiátrica del Sur y Este de España*. 23(3), 305–310.

Diaz, J. (1990). Pubertad y somatización. *Revista de la Sociedad Española del Rorschach y Métodos Proyectivos*. 3, 41–52.

Diego, R. (1989). Psicodiagnóstico discriminativo del trastorno antisocial de la personalidad. Tesis Doctoral. Universidad Pontificia de Salamanca.

Forns, M., Aznar, J.a., & Fogued, M. T. (1985). Estudio del estilo cognitivo en el Test de Rorschach. *Anuario de Psicología*. 1(32), 117–141.

Galan, F. (1988). Estudio de un grupo de obesos mediante el Test de Rorschach. *Revista de la Sociedad Española del Rorschach y Métodos Proyectivos*. 1, 39–46.

Hierro, M. D. (1984). Estudio de la enuresis a través del psicodiagnóstico de Rorschach. Tesis Doctoral. Universidad Central de Barcelona.

Hierro, M. D. (1986). Rasgos de personalidad en sujetos enuréticos. *Universitas Tarraconensis*. 6(2), 195–203.

Hierro, M. D., & Palavecino, J. (1985). El proceso de psicodiagnóstico. Estudio de un caso. Diseño de n=1. *Universitas Tarraconensis*. 7(2), 179–188.

Insua, A., & Loza, S. (1988). Evaluación de los signos de organicidad, según Piotrowsky, en el Rorschach de pacientes con un comienzo de demencia. *Acta Psiquiátrica y Psicológica de América Latina*. 34(3), 243–250.

Jimenez, C. (1987). El deterioro en pacientes esquizofrénicos, aspectos formales y tipos de deterioro. Tesis Doctoral. Universidad de Córdoba.

Jimenez, F. (1984). Sintomatología afectivo-angustiosa y agresiva en el psicodiagnóstico de Rorschach y Láminas Proyectivas. Tesis Doctoral. Universidad Pontificia de Salamanca.

Jimenez, F. (1990). *Introducción al Psicodiagnóstico del Rorschach y Láminas Proyectivas*. Salamanca. Amaru

Jimenez, F., & Diego, R. (1991a). *Rorschach y Láminas Proyectivas: Teoría e Investigación*. Salamanca. Amaru.

Jimenez, F., & Diego, R. (1991b). Trastorno antisocial de la personalidad a través del Test de Rorschach. *Revista de Psicología General y Aplicada*. 44(1), 75–86.

Jimenez, F. et al. (1990). Los contenidos humanos y animales en el psicodiagnóstico de Rorschach: una aportación desde las láminas proyectivas. *II Congreso del Colegio Oficial de Psicólogos*. 7, 336–342.

Jimenez, M. A., & Perez, P. (1984). Transexualismo femenino: Experiencia clínica. *Revista de Psicoterapia y Psicosomática*. 9, 69–105.

Larraz, L., & Valero, A. (1988). Respuestas populares al Test de Rorschach en población española. Muestra de Barcelona. *Revista de la Sociedad Española del Rorschach y Métodos Proyectivos*. 1, 47–54.

Leon, J., & Valencia, J.a. (1986). Perspectiva comprensiva de los aspectos neuropsicológicos en niños con síndrome de déficit de atención con hiperactividad a través de los resultados obtenidos en el Test de Rorschach. (Aportación preliminar). *Psiquis*. 7(6), 57–64.

Marquez, M. O. (1985). Procesamiento de información en Rorschach. Tesis Doctoral. Universidad Autónoma de Madrid.

Marquez, M. O. (1986). Estudio bibliométrico sobre el Test de Rorschach. *Revista de Historia de la Psicología*. 7(3), 71–82.

Marquez, M. O., & Fernandez-Ballesteros, R. (1988). Procesamiento icónico de los estímulos del Rorschach. *Evaluación Psicológica*. 4(2), 223–238.

Marquez, M. O., Fernandez-Ballesteros, R., & Rubio, V. (1985). Procesamiento icónico y aplicación estándar del Rorschach. *Revista de Psicología General y Aplicada*. 40(5), 923–943.

Martinez, M., & Navarro, M. (1985). Un caso de esquizofrenia esquizoafectiva en un paciente de 14 años. *Folia Neuropsiquiátrica*. 20(3), 361–366.

Mateo, E. (1986). Aplicación do Test Rorschach no seguimento dun tratamento médico-psicoterapéutico. *I Congreso Profesional de Psicoloxia Galicia, Edidos de Intervención en Psicoloxia*. 53–57.

Mateo, M. (1988). Estudio de las limitaciones de la prueba de Rorschach en aplicación colectiva y de la utilización de aquellos componentes no afectados para la elaboración de un programa psicométrico para selección de personal. *I Congreso Iberoamericano y Tercero Nacional de Psicología del Trabajo y de las Organizaciones*. 5, 1–6.

Megias, E., & Mas, C. (1986). Vivencia del cuerpo: análisis percepto-cognitivo. *Psicomotricidad*. 23, 78–86.

Ortiz, P. (1990a). El Test de Rorschach según el Sistema Comprensivo de Exner: Administración y valoración de respuestas. En Avila, A. (Ed.) *Evaluación Psicológica II*. Universidad Complutense de Madrid.

Ortiz, P. (1990b). El Test de Rorschach según el Sistema Comprensivo de Exner: Bases para la interpretación. En Avila, A. (Ed.) *Evaluación Psicológica II*. Universidad Complutense de Madrid.

Ortiz, P. (1990c). Estudio del autoconcepto en sujetos parapléjicos varones. Tesis Doctoral publicada. Ed. Universidad Complutense.

Ortiz, P. (1991). Evaluación del autoconcepto en parapléjicos a través del Rorschach. *Revista de la Sociedad Española del Rorschach y Métodos Proyectivos*. 39–49.

Ortiz, P. et al. (1990). Consideraciones acerca de la repercusión de la paraplejia en la imagen corporal. *II Congreso del Colegio Oficial de Psicólogos*. 7, 328–332.

Perez, P. et al. (1991). Perversión y psicosis. *Revista de la Sociedad Española del Rorschach y Métodos Proyectivos*. 4, 18–32.

Perez, J. M. (1985). *El Rorschach en la psicopatología actual*. Madrid. Author.

Portuondo, J. A. (1989). *El psicodiagóstico de Rorschach clásico y psicoanalítico*. Barcelona. Psique.

Quiroga, M. A. (1988a). El estilo cognitivo Dependencia-Independencia de Campo: Un estudio diferencial a través de los perfiles del Rorschach. Tesis Doctoral publicada. Ed. Universidad Complutense.

Quiroga, M. A. (1988b). Correlatos cognitivos y no cognitivos de la Reflexividad-Impulsividad: Un estudio diferencial a través de los perfiles del Rorschach. *Investigaciones Psicológicas*. 5, 125–157.

Rodriguez Linde, E., & Herrero, J. J. (1986). Caso clínico: alopecia y psicosomática. *Folia Neuropsiquiátrica del Sur y Este de España*. 21(2), 331–334.

Rodriguez Sutil, C. (1984). Dependencia-Independencia de campo: Psicodiagnóstico y Psicopatología. *Anuario de Psicología*, 3(3), 259-272.

Rodriguez Sutil, C. (1990). Situación actual del Test de Rorschach. *Anuario de Psicología*. 2(45), 88-99.

Ros, M. (1988). Aspectos estructurales que muestran un grupo de personalidades cuyo rol laboral y social es el mando o responsabilidad última. *Revista de la Sociedad Española del Rorschach y Métodos Proyectivos*. 1, 55-62.

Ros, M. (1989). The use and importance of the symbol in the Rorschach Test. *British Journal of Projective Psychology*. 34(1), 2-27.

Ros, M. (1990). La vulnerabilidad del test de Rorschach y del Mmpi en relación a la depresión simulada. Tesis Doctoral. Universidad Central de Barcelona.

Ros, M. (1991). La fiabilidad del Test de Rorschach en los peritajes jurídicos. *Rorschachiana*. XVII, 215-217.

Rovira, F. (1990). El Test de Rorschach en adolescentes con problemas de adaptación. Tesis Doctoral. Universidad Central de Barcelona.

Rubio, R. (1985). Aspectos de la estructura básica de la personalidad en la tercera edad según el Sistema Comprensivo propuesto por Exner. *Folia Neuropsiquiátrica*. 20(3), 327-342.

Ruiz, C. (1986). El Rorschach en los síndromes depresivos. *Folia Neuropsiquiátrica del Sur y Este de España*. 21(2), 255-261.

Ruiz, C. (1987). Estudio del Test de Rorschach y la referencia personal simbólica en los estados depresivos. *Folia Neuropsiquiátrica del Sur y Este de España*. 22(1), 99-114.

Ruiz, M. et al. (1987). Diagnóstico de las esquizofrenias mediante la técnica del Rorschach. *Folia Neuropsiquiátrica del Sur y Este de España*. 22(3), 289-312.

Ruiz, M. et al. (1989). Evaluación psicodiagnóstica de las esquizofrenias paranoides mediante el Rorschach conceptual. *Folia Neuropsiquiátrica del Sur y Este de España*. 42(3), 331-341.

Ruiz, M.E. (1984). Características psicosociales de los delincuentes juveniles. Tesis Doctoral. Universidad de Murcia.

Rus, P. (1986). La personalidad del enfermo coronario. *Folia Neuropsiquiátrica del Sur y Este de España*. 21(1), 127-135.

Salamero, C. et al. (1990). Personalidad y organicidad en esquizofrenia residual mediante el psicodiagnóstico de Rorschach. *Psiquis*. 11(10), 29-38.

Sendin, C. (1987a). La estructura del Test de Rorschach. *Rorschachiana*. XVI, 152-157.

Sendin, C. (1987b). Datos normativos del Test de Rorschach en sujetos españoles. *Rorschachiana*. XVI, 264.

Sendin, C. (1987c). El Rorschach en evaluación de tratamientos. *Rorschachiana*. XVI, 252.

Sendin, C. (1988). Datos normativos al Test de Rorschach. *Revista de la Academia Lombarda de Rorschach*. 1, 98-104.

Sendin, C. (1989). La estructura factorial del Test de Rorschach. Tesis Doctoral. Universidad Complutense de Madrid.

Sendin, C. (1990a). Factorial analysis of Rorschach Test: Intergroup comparison. *Rorschachiana*. XVII, 85–90.

Sendin, C. (1990b). Estructura factorial del Test de Rorschach: Comparación inter-grupos. *Clínica y Salud*. 1(2), 143–152.

Sendin, C. & Garcia, C. (1987). El Rorschach en evaluación de tratamientos. *Ror-schachiana*, XVI, 252.

Tuset, A. (1990). Análisis de las respuestas al Test de Rorschach de un grupo de sujetos afectados de un primer infarto de miocardio. Tesis Doctoral. Universidad Central de Barcelona.

Tuset, A., & Estany, T. (1990). La respuesta a la IVE evaluada a trvés del Rorschach. *II Congreso del Colegio Oficial de Psicólogos*. 7, 332–336.

Valencia, J. A., and Leon, J. (1987). Estructura cognitiva de los niños hiperactivos y de sus madres. *Psiquis*. 8(9–10), 35–44.

Valsuarez-Llanos, M. (1984). Un estudio del inconsciente en la tercera edad. *Psiquis*. 5(4), 59–70.

Vargas, A. et al.(1984). La personalidad del heroinómano. *Psicopatología*. 4(1), 39–47.

Vazquez, A., & Benavente, J. L. (1987). Elementos patológicos de la personalidad de las mujeres de los alcohólicos en el psicodiagnóstico de Rorschach. *Folia Neuropsiquiátrica del Sur y Este de España*. 22(2), 185–198.

Velilla, M., Bonals, A., & Miravete, P. (1984). Los tests de manchas de tinta en la anorexia mental. *Comunicación Psiquiátrica*. 11, 141–154.

Vives, M. (1984). Indices Rorschach en esquizofrénicos crónicos versus esquizofrénicos agudos. Tesis Doctoral. Universidad Central de Barcelona.

Vives, M. (1986). Esquizofrenia de exacerbación aguda: Estudio piloto con psicodiagnóstico de Rorschach. *Universitas Tarraconensis*. 8(2), 157–165.

Vives, M. (1985a). El Rorschach en el diagnpostico de la esquizofrenia crónica. *Cuadernos de Psicología*. 9/1, 2 época, 99–110.

Vives, M. (1985b). Coincidencia diagnóstica entre los instrumentos RDC y Rorschach. *Universitas Tarraconensis*. 7(1), 101–105.

Vives, M. (1989). *El Rorschach, instrumento de diagnóstico y pronóstico en la diferenciación de la esquizofrenia*. Barcelona. PPU.

Vives, M. (1991). Estudio cualitativo-cuantitativo de la esquizofrenia de exacerbación aguda. *Rorschachiana*. XVII, 241–247.

Vizcarro, C. (1986). Utilidad del Rorschach en el diagnóstico de la esquizofrenia. *Evaluación Psicológica*. 2(4), 79–88.

Object Relations Theory and the Rorschach

Paul M. Lerner

Asheville, NC, USA

Psychoanalysis is not a closed, tightly knit, totally integrated theory of personality. Rather, it is a mosaic, a loose fitting composite of several complementary, internally consistent submodels, each of which furnishes concepts and formulations for understanding important aspect of personality development and functioning. The submodels commonly identified include drive theory, structural theory, object relations theory, and self theory (Pine, 1990; P. Lerner, 1991).

Based on the pioneering work of Rapaport (Gill, 1967), who was the first theorist to integrate the Rorschach with psychoanalytic theory, each of these submodels has served as a valuable conceptual base for informing clinical assessment as well as for generating research with respect to personality and psychopathology.

In this paper I will review and integrate a select group of research endeavors which have attempted to operationalize and investigate concepts and formulations arising from object relations theory. The specific concepts to be reviewed include defense, object representations, and developmental object relations. I have chosen these topics because they are basic and timely and because they represent areas in which investigators have devised, for research purposes, innovative, conceptually based scoring systems.

Although a comprehensive discussion of object relations theory is beyond the scope of this article, in general, this submodel or perspective focuses on the complex interactions among early formative interpersonal relationships; the level and quality of internal psychological structures including thought processes, defense organization, and the representational world; and the nature of ongoing interpersonal relations and the ways they are internalized and become part of the personality.

Defense

The concept of defense has been a cornerstone of psychoanalytic theory (Hoffer, 1968; Leeuw, 1971; Madison, 1961; Rapaport, 1958). Although Freud's (1915/1957, 1923/1961, 1926/1959) view of defense changed over time, the conception he presented in *The Ego and the Id* (1923/1961) eventually became the basis of his structural theory of personality and of the development of ego psychology (A. Freud, 1936; Rapaport, 1958; Reich, 1972).

The most dramatic and innovative changes in the concept of defense have arisen from the British School of Object Relations beginning with the writings of Melanie Klein (1975). Klein fundamentally reconceptualized defense by suggesting that such mechanisms not only regulate affects and drives, but are also related to the effects on intimacy and cognition of the experience, organization, and internalization of object relations. For Klein, defenses protect the ego from overwhelming sensations, and, as well, are nondefensive principles of infantile mental life.

An effort to integrate Klein's object relational view of defense with earlier, more traditional formulations, is represented in the work of Kernberg (1975), and, in particular, his structural concept of levels of defensive organization. Kernberg proposed a hierarchical organization of levels of character pathology related directly to defensive functioning and developmental level of internalized object relations. For Kernberg, internalized object relations are organized on the basis of specific defensive structures. As part of this model he systematically defined and outlined the more primitive defenses described by Klein, clarified the distinction between splitting and repression, and related specific defenses to level of and type of psychopathology.

Kernberg identified two overall levels of defensive organization of the ego associated with pre-oedipal and oedipal pathology respectively. At the lower level splitting is the basic defensive operation bolstered through the related defenses of low level denial, primitive idealization, primitive devaluation, and projective identification. At a higher developmental level associated with oedipal pathology, repression replaces splitting as the major defense and is accompanied by the related defensive operations of undoing, intellectualization, rationalization, and higher level forms of denial and projection.

Based upon Kernberg's theoretical conceptualizations of defense, Lerner and Lerner (1980) developed a Rorschach scoring manual de-

46

signed to evaluate the specific defensive operations presumed to characterize the developmentally lower level of defensive functioning.

The scoring manual is divided into sections on the basis of the specific defenses of splitting, devaluation, idealization, denial, and projective identification. Within each section the defense is defined, Rorschach indices of the defense are presented, and clinical examples are offered. The sections on devaluation, idealization, and denial call for an identification of the defense as well as a ranking of the defense on a continuum of high versus low order. In keeping with Kernberg's contention that these defenses organize and reflect the internal object world and with the empirical relationship found between human responses on the Rorschach and quality of object relating (Blatt & Lerner, 1983), the system involves a systematic appraisal of the human figure response.

Results from various studies (Lerner & Lerner, 1980; Lerner, Sugarman, & Gaughran, 1981; Gacono, 1988; Van-Der Keshet, 1988) indicate that the reliability of the scoring system as judged by level of interrater agreement is particularly high for an inkblot measure.

In accord with theoretical formulations, early studies employing the scale sought to demonstrate its efficacy in distinguishing borderline patients from other diagnostic entities. In a series of studies (Lerner & Lerner, 1980; Lerner, Sugarman, & Gaughran, 1981; Collins, 1983; Farris, 1988; Lerner, Albert, & Walsh, 1987) it has been consistently demonstrated that patients organized at a borderline level manifest a discernible defensive structure different in kind from those of psychotic, neurotic, and narcissistic patients. Although the specific pattern of defenses among groups of borderline patients may vary, in virtually all studies the theoretical centrality accorded splitting has been supported.

Later studies used the scale to evaluate the defensive structure among other types of clinical groups (i. e., eating disorder patients, antisocial personality, gender disturbed children) assumed to have a borderline personality structure. For example, in one group of these studies (Brouillette, 1987; Piran & Lerner, 1988; Van-Der Keshet, 1988) scale scores distinguished eating disorder patients from normal controls. Van-Der Keshet's (1988) investigation highlighted the role of idealization and added to its conceptual meaning. Brouillette's (1987) study was unique in that it dealt with not only anorexic patients, but with their mothers as well. Results involving differing defensive patterning between subtypes of eating disorder patients were equivocal and sample specific.

Cooper and his colleagues (Cooper & Aronow, 1986; Cooper, Perry, & Aronow, 1988) also developed a Rorschach scale designed, in part, to assess primitive defenses. Drawing on the theoretical propositions of Winnicott (1953), Kohut (1977), Kernberg (1975), and Stolorow and Lachmann (1980), Cooper's scale sought to integrate object relations theory, Kohut's notions of narcissism, and Stolorow and Lachmann's concepts of developmental arrest and structural deficiency. Broader in scope than the Lerner and Lerner Scale, this system involves the assessment of 15 defenses including the more primitive defenses of devaluation, omnipotence, primitive idealization, projection, projective identification, and splitting.

Like the Lerner and Lerner system, Cooper's instrument relies heavily on the analysis of Rorschach content. However, Cooper's basic unit of analysis extends beyond the human figure response to encompass a broad array of contents (animal responses, inanimate movement, etc.).

In a comprehensive concurrent validity study (Lerner, Albert, & Walsh, 1987), both scales were found useful in distinguishing borderline patients from other diagnostic entities. At the same time, however, perhaps owing to their different conceptual starting points and their somewhat differing ways of operationally defining specific defenses, scores on the Cooper Scale seemed more effective in distinguishing among higher functioning outpatients, whereas scores on the Lerner and Lerner Scale appeared more effective in differentiating poorer functioning inpatients.

A second concept emerging from object relations theory which has gained increased currency in the Rorschach literature is "object representation." Defined broadly, object representation refers to the conscious and unconscious mental schemata, including cognitive, affective, and experiential components of objects encountered in reality (Blatt & Lerner, 1983). Beginning as vague, diffuse, variable sensorimotor experiences of pleasure and unpleasure, they gradually expand and develop into differentiated, consistent, relatively realistic representations of the self and the object world. Earlier forms of representation are based more on action sequences associated with need gratification, intermediate forms are based on specific perceptual features, and higher forms are more symbolic and conceptual. Whereas these schemata evolve from and are intertwined with the developmental internalization of object relations and ego functions (Mahler, Pine, & Bergmann, 1975), the developing representations provide a new organization for experiencing object relations.

A major approach to the study and assessment of object representations is represented in the work of Blatt and his colleagues. Building on their initial investigation of boundary disturbances (Blatt & Ritzler, 1974; Brenneis, 1971), Blatt, Brenneis, Schimek, and Glick (1976) developed a highly comprehensive Rorschach manual for assessing object representations. The system calls for the scoring of human responses in terms of the developmental principles of differentiation, articulation, and integration. Within each of these areas categories were established along a continuum based on developmental levels. Differentiation refers to the type of figure perceived, whether the figure is quasi-human detail, human detail, quasi-human, or a full human figure. For articulation, responses are scored on the basis of the number and types of attributes ascribed to the figure. Integration of the response is scored in three ways: the degree of internality of the action, the degree of integration of the interaction with another object, and the integration of the object and its action. Responses are also scored along a content dimension of benevolence – malevolence.

In an initial study (Blatt, et al., 1976) the scoring system was applied to the Rorschach records of normal subjects on four separate occasions over a 20 year period. In this longitudinal study of normal development the authors found a marked increase, over time, in the number of accurately perceived, well-articulated full human figures involved in appropriate, integrated, positive, and meaningful interaction.

In the second part of this initial study, the records of the normal subjects obtained at age 17 were compared with the Rorschachs of a hospitalized sample of disturbed adolescents and young adults. In comparison with the normals, patients gave human figures that were significantly more inaccurately perceived, distorted, and seen as inert or engaged in unmotivated, incongruent, nonspecific, and malevolent activity. The combined results of this study lent strong support to the construct validity of the concept of object representation and the manual devised to assess it.

The relationship between level of object representation and nature of psychopathology has been well demonstrated in studies by Blatt and Lerner (1983), Lerner and St. Peter (1984) and Stuart, Westen, Lohr, Benjamin, Becker, Vorus, and Silk (1990).

Blatt and Lerner (1983) applied the object representation scale to the Rorschach records of several patients, each of whom was independently selected as a prototypic example of a specific clinical disorder. The authors not only found a unique quality of object representation for each of the clinical entities, but their findings, based on Rorschach data, were remarkably congruent with clinical expectations. For example, in a narcissistic-borderline patient the object representations were found to progressively deteriorate either over time or with stress. Initially, the representations were accurate, well-differentiated, and appropriately articulated; however, this gave way to representations that were inaccurately perceived, inappropriately articulated, and seen as part rather than whole figures.

Lerner and St. Peter (1984) applied the Blatt scale to the Rorschachs of independently diagnosed outpatient neurotic and borderline subjects as well as hospitalized borderline and schizophrenic patients. Analyzing the results separately for perceptually accurate and inaccurate responses, the authors found that schizophrenic patients produced significantly fewer accurate responses and portrayed human figures at lower developmental levels than the other three groups. This impairment in the representation of objects serves as a distinguishing factor between schizophrenic and borderline patients and is consistent with previous clinical and research reports.

Unexpectedly, however, the inpatient borderline sample functioned at the highest developmental level of differentiation, articulation, and integration for inaccurate responses, and, in general, produced more inaccurate responses in these categories than the other three groups. The results, particularly in regard to the hospitalized borderline group, highlighted the content dimension of object representations as being a critical discriminatory variable. The inpatient borderline sample produced the most responses with malevolent content and were the only group to offer inaccurately perceived malevolent responses. Whereas only 25% of all other subjects offered malevolent human responses, the inpatient borderlines attributed malevolency to 42% of their human responses and to 94% of their quasi-human responses. These findings clearly illustrate the enormous difficulty these patients experience in managing aggression within interpersonal relationships.

Finally, Stuart et al. (1990) used Blatt's Scale to compare the object representations of borderline patients with those of inpatient depressives and normal controls. In contrast with the other groups, an analysis of the object representations of the borderline patients indicated that these individuals view relationships in need-gratifying ways; attribute the causes of peoples' behavior, thoughts, and feelings idiosyncratically; tend to represent the self and others pathologically, which at times involves infusing their representations with fantasy elaborations resulting in representations that are hyper-complex and distorted; and experience their object world as highly malevolent.

50

Developmental Object Relations

With a shift in emphases in psychoanalytic theory toward a view of object relations from a developmental perspective, the past decade has witnessed the emergence of several psychoanalytically based Rorschach scales devised to evaluate quality of object relations along a developmental continuum. To varying degrees these scales have been conceptually rooted in Mahler's (Mahler, Pine, & Bergmann, 1975) theory of separation-individuation.

Representative of these newer conceptually based scales in the work of Coonerty (1986). Using Mahler's descriptions as a guideline, Coonerty developed a scale for identifying and categorizing Rorschach responses reflective of concerns and issues associated with the pre-separation stage and each of the phases of the separation-individuation process.

Referable to the pre-separation phase are internal responses (such as blood, lungs, heart) and responses lacking boundaries (such as fabulized combination). Rorschach imagery reflective of merging, engulfment, and hatching is taken as indicative of concerns arising from the early differentiation subphase of separation-individuation. Themes related to the practicing subphase involve narcissistic issues; thus, illustrative Rorschach content includes mirroring responses, pairing responses, omnipotent responses, and insignificant creative responses. Responses indicative of rapprochement issues include figures separating or coming together with resulting damage to one or both, figures engaged in a push-pull struggle, figures whose form changes, figures whose affect changes, and figures enmeshed and unable to separate.

Coonerty applied the scale to the Rorschach protocols of 50 borderline patients and 50 schizophrenic patients. Subjects were all adult patients, 18 to 65 years of age, who met DSM-III criteria based upon a detailed initial screening evaluation. Reliability of the scale was found to be 96% agreement between two raters. As predicted, the borderline group offered more separation-individuation themes than did the schizophrenic group, whereas the schizophrenics provided more pre-separation themes.

Van-Der Keshet (1988) applied Coonerty's (1986) scale to the Rorschach records of clinical anorexics, anorexic ballet students, nonanorexic ballet students, and a normal control group. The clinical anorexic group was further subdivided into those patients manifesting restrictive characteristics and those exhibiting bulimic symptoms. A comparison of the various groups on the scale revealed several interesting findings. Although no main effect was found among the groups on the preseparation scale, several significant findings were obtained on the separation-individuation scores. Bulimic anorexics produced significantly more engulfment responses than did any of the other groups. Mirroring responses distinguished the anorexic ballet students from each of the other groups. The controls had significantly fewer rapprochement responses than the other four groups. The overall pattern of results not only lent construct validity to Coonerty's Scale but also demonstrated the measure's sensitivity to significant dynamic configurations associated with specific clinical groups.

Conclusion

Psychoanalytic theory has always been in a constant state of evolution and change. As a consequence of more recent shifts, basic concepts, such as defense, that had been understood in exclusively structural and economic terms, are now being reformulated to take into account the decisive impact of object relations.

These shifts in theory, in turn, have provided new and stimulating conceptualizations that have served to broaden the theoretical basis for the Rorschach's clinical and research application.

In this article I have selectively sampled rather than exhaustively reviewed studies which have attempted to assess aspects of object relations based upon psychoanalytic object relations theory. The specific concepts discussed include defense, object representations, and developmental object relations. Studies were selected which employed relatively recent, innovative, conceptually based Rorschach scales.

I have drawn on an increasingly sophisticated Rorschach literature that combines timely psychoanalytic concepts with research methodologies of substantial rigor to generate sturdy empirical findings.

Paul M. Lerner

Résumé

La psychanalyse englobe divers modèles (théorie des pulsions, théorie métapsychologique, théorie des relations d'objet, théorie du self) qui essayent tous de comprendre et d'expliquer des aspects significatifs du développement et du fonctionnement de la personnalité. Par ailleurs, chacun de ces modèles offre une base conceptuelle susceptible de simultanément enrichir l'évaluation clinique et générer des recherches en matière de personnalité et de psychopathologie.

Dans cet article, nous passons en revue un groupe d'études choisies, ayant utilisé le Rorschach pour opérationaliser et approfondir des concepts, issus de la théorie des relations d'objet et influencés par cette dernière. Les concepts examinés ici sont ceux de défense, de relation d'objet et de relation d'objet développementale.

Ces concepts furent choisis, d'une part parce qu'ils forment la base de la théorie psychanalytique, d'autre part parce qu'ils représentent des domaines dans lesquels les chercheurs ont imaginé avec créativité des systèmes de cotation innovateurs, conceptuellement fondés et valides. Les systèmes de cotation discutés ici regroupent l'Echelle des Défenses de P. Lerner et H. Lerner, l'Echelle de Représentation d'Objet de Blatt et l'Echelle d'Evaluation de la Séparation-Individuation de Coonerty.

Les résultats de nombre de recherches ont servi à étayer la validité conceptuelle de chacune de ces échelles. Par exemple, l'échelle des Défenses des Lerner a été jugée efficace pour différencier des patients borderline d'autres entités diagnostiques et pour évaluer la constellation défensive de certains groupes cliniques (tels que des patients présentant des troubles alimentaires), supposés présenter une organisation de personnalité borderline. Les résultats concernant l'échelle de Blatt ont démontré, à plusieurs reprises, l'importance de la relation entre le niveau de représentation d'objet et la nature de la psychopathologie. Par ailleurs, cette échelle s'est avérée particulièrement utile pour circonscrire la coloration très spécifique des relations d'objet cher lez patients borderline. L'échelle de Coonerty a été judicieusement appliquée pour appuyer empiriquement des théories cliniques qui postulent le rôle clef des efforts de séparation-individuation dans la dynamique du vécu des patients borderline.

Dans leur ensemble, les études commentées ici s'inscrivent dans le cadre d'une littérature Rorschach en empansion, alliant des concepts psychanalytiques de base à des méthodologies de recherche suffisamment rigoureuses pour pouvoir générer des résultats empiriques solides.

Resumen

El Psicoanálisis consiste en varios submodelos (i. e. teoría de la pulsión. teoría estructural, teoría de las relaciones objetales, teoría del sí-mismo), cada uno de los cuales busca comprender y explicar aspectos significativos del desarrollo y el funcionamiento de la personalidad. Cada submodelo ha proporcionado igualmente una base conceptual, tanto para guiar la evaluación clínica, como para generar investigaciones relacionadas con la personalidad y la psicopatología.

En este trabajo resumo una selección de estudios, que han utilizado el Rorschach para operacionalizar e investigar los conceptos que surgen, o que han sido influenciados, por la teoría de las relaciones objetales. Entre los conceptos específicos revisados se incluyen: defensa, representación de objeto y relaciones objetales en el marco del desarrollo evolutivo.

Se escogieron estos conceptos debido a que constituyen aspectos básicos de la teoría psicoanalítica, y representan áreas en las cuales los investigadores han diseñado creativamente sistemas de valoración conceqtualmente basados, innovadores y confiables. Los sistemas específicos de valoración que se discuten son: la Escala de Defensa de P. Lerner y H. Lerner, el concepto de Escala de Objeto de Blatt, y la Escala para evaluar Separación-Individuación de Coonerty.

Hallazgos provenientes de varios estudios han servido para sustentar la validez de constructo de cada una de estas escalas. Por ejemplo, la Escala de Defensa de Lerner ha resultado efectiva para distinguir los pacientes borderline de otras entidades diagnósticas, y para evaluar la estructura defensiva de ciertas grupos clínicos (i. e., pacientes con trastornos de la alimentación), de los cuales se asume que presentan una estructura borderline de la personalidad. Los resultados obtenidos con la Escala de Blatt han demostrado repetidamente la importancia de la relación entre el nivel de representación objetal y la naturaleza de la psicopatología. Además, esta Escala ha resultado muy valiosa para delinear la cualidad específica de la relación de objets en los pacientes borderline. La escale de Coonerty ha sido de utilidad en proveer un sustento empírico para las teorias clínicas que asientan el rol fundamental desempeñado, en la dinámica de los pacientes borderline, por les luchas en torno a la separación-individuación.

Colectivamente, los estudios revisados son parte de una literatura sobre el Rorschach que viene incrementándose, la cual, para generar hallazgos empiricos sólidos, combina conceptos psicoanalíticos fondamentales con metodologías de investigación substancialmente rigurosas.

References

Blatt, S., Brenneis, C., Schimek, J., & Glick, M. (1976). Normal development and psychopathological impairment of the concept of the object on the Rorschach. *Journal of Abnormal Psychology, 85*, 364–373.

Blatt, S., & Lerner, H. (1983). The psychological assessment of object representation. *Journal of Personality Assessment, 47*, 7–28.

Blatt, S., & Ritzler, B. (1974). Thought disorder and boundary disturbances in psychosis. *Journal of Consulting and Clinical Psychology, 42*, 370–381.

Brouillette, C. (1987). A Rorschach assessment of the character structure of anorexia nervosa and bulimia patients and their mothers. Unpublished doctoral dissertation, University of Toronto.

Collins, R. (1983). Rorschach correlates of borderline personality. Unpublished doctoral dissertation, University of Toronto.

Coonerty, S. (1986). An exploration of separation-individuation themes in the borderline personality disorder. *Journal of Personality Assessment, 50*, 501–511.

Cooper, S., & Aronow, D. (1986). An object relations view of the borderline defenses: A review. In M. Kissen (Ed.), *Assessing object relations phenomena* (pp. 143–171). New York: International Universities Press.

Cooper, S., Perry, J., & Aronow, D. (1988). An empirical approach to the study of defense mechanisms: I. Reliability and preliminary validity of the Rorschach defense scale. *Journal of Personality Assessment, 52*, 187–203.

Farris, M. (1988). Differential diagnosis of borderline and narcissistic personality disorders. In H. Lerner & P. Lerner (Eds.), *Primitive mental states and the Rorschach* (pp. 299–338). Madison, CT: International Universities Press.

Freud, A. (1936). *The ego and the mechanisms of defense.* New York: International Universities Press.

Freud, S. (1957). Instincts and their vicissitudes. In J. Strachey (Ed. & Trans.), *The standard edition of the complete psychological works of Sigmund Freud* (Vol. 14, pp. 109–140). London: Hogarth. (Original work published 1915).

Freud, S. (1961). The ego and the id. In J. Strachey (Ed. & Trans.), The standard edition of the complete psychological works of *Sigmund Freud* (Vol. 19, pp. 3–66). London: Hogarth. (Original work published 1923).

Freud, S. (1959). Inhibitions, symptoms and anxiety. In J. Strachey (Ed. & Trans.), *The standard edition of the complete psychological works of Sigmund Freud* (Vol. 20, pp. 87–174). London: Hogarth. (Original work published 1926).

Gacono, C. (1988). A Rorschach analysis of object relations and defensive structure and their relationship to narcissism and psychopathy in a group of antisocial offenders. Unpublished doctoral dissertation, United States International University.

Gill, M. (1967). *The collected papers of David Rapaport*, New York: Basic Books.

Hoffer, W. (1968). Notes on the theory of defense. *Psychoanalytic Study of the Child, 23*, 178–188.

Kernberg, O. (1975). *Borderline conditions and pathological narcissism.* New York: Jason Aronson.

Klein, M. (1975). *Love, guilt, reparation and other works 1921–1945.* London: Hogarth.

Kohut, H. (1977). *The restoration of the self.* New York: International Universities Press.

Leeuw, P. (1971). On the development of the concept of defense. *International Journal of Psychoanalysis, 52*, 51–58.

Lerner, H., Albert, C., & Walsh, M. (1987). The Rorschach assessment of borderline defenses. *Journal of Personality Assessment, 51*, 344–354.

Lerner, H., & St. Peter, S. (1984). Patterns of object relations in neurotic, borderline, and schizophrenic patients. *Psychiatry, 37*, 77–91.

Lerner, H. , Sugarman, A., & Gaughran, J. (1981). Borderline and schizophrenic patients: A comparative study of defensive structure. *Journal of Nervous & Mental Disease, 169*, 705–711.

Lerner, P. (1991). *Psychoanalytic theory and the Rorschach.* Hillsdale, NJ: Analytic Press.

Lerner, P., & Lerner, H. (1980). Rorschach assessment of primitive defenses in borderline personality structure. In J. Kwawer, H. Lerner, P. Lerner, & A. Sugarman (Eds.), *Borderline phenomena and the Rorschach test* (pp. 257–274). New York: International Universities Press.

Madison, P. (1961). *Freud's concept of repression and defense, its theoretical and observational language.* Minneapolis: University of Minnesota Press.

Mahler, M., Pine, F., & Bergmann, A. (1975). *The psychological birth of the human infant.* New York: Basic Books.

Pine, F. (1990). *Drive, ego, object and self.* New York: Basic Books.

Piran, N., & Lerner, P. (1988). Rorschach assessment of anorexia nervosa and bulimia. In C. Spielberger & J. Butcher (Eds.), *Advances in Personality Assessment, 7*, 77–102.

Rapaport, D. (1958). An historical review of psychoanalytic ego psychology. In M. Gill (Ed.), *The collected papers of David Rapaport* (pp. 745–757). New York: Basic Books.

Reich, W. (1972). *Character analysis.* New York: Farrar, Strauss, & Ciroux.

Stolorow, R., & Lachmann, F. (1980). *The psychoanalysis of developmental arrest.* New York: International Universities Press.

Stuart, J., Westen, D., Lohr, N., Benjamin, J., Becker, S., Vorus, N., & Silk, K. (1990). Object relations in borderline, depressives, and normals: An examination of human responses on the Rorschach. *Journal of Personality Assessment, 55,* 296–318.

Van-Der Keshet, Y. (1988). *Anorexic patients and ballet students: A Rorschach analysis.* Unpublished doctoral dissertation, University of Toronto.

Winnicott, D. (1953). Transitional objects and transitional phenomena. *International Journal of Psychoanalysis, 34,* 89–97.

The Parallel Inkblot Plates Developed by S. Parisi and P. Pes

Salvatore Parisi

Scuola Romana Rorschach, Rome, Italy

The Parallel Inkblot Plates, a result of 15 years of painstaking work, constitute the approach of the Scuola Romana Rorschach to a vexing problem that Rorschach researchers have up until now been only partially successful in resolving. We refer to the fact that we have not had a satisfactory series of Plates that could substitute adequately for the original inkblots in cases when the originals cannot be used. Specifically, the use of the Rorschach Inkblot Plates may not be advisable in two circumstances.

The first of these circumstances occurs then it is necessary to re-examine the same subject, that is, to do a re-test with the Rorschach. A re-test with the Rorschach may not be valid for diagnostic use, because of the likelihood that taking the test will generate some processes of learning and memory. Taking the Rorschach is a special experience, full of vivid and intense emotions that are not easily "metabolized" and are unlikely to be forgotten except after a long interval of time. It is our belief that aspects of this experience are likely to make a continuing impression on the subject, in such a way as to limit the validity of results obtained on re-testing. Accordingly, necessity for re-examination is an ideal condition for being able to use alternate plates that differ from but have the same basic characteristics as the original Rorschach inkblots.

A second circumstance that calls for the utilization of plates occurs when we suspect that the subject has received "instructions" in how to fake the test and give answers that will obscure the true diagnosis. The possibility that subjects will attempt to give deceptive or misleading responses is increasing in today's times as the Rorschach test is being used with increasing frequency in such important areas as selecting personnel and solving legal disputes.

At this point it is necessary to define what is meant by a "Parallel" of the Rorschach plates. By this we mean a series of plates that, with respect to their most distinctive and interpretively significant features, are similar to the plates developed 70 years ago by Hermann Rorschach, but that differ from the original plates in various minor or unimportant ways. Rorschach himself subscribed to the necessity of having a Parallel series. In his *Psychodiagnostics* (1921/1942) he concluded that memory factors "warp the result" if the test is repeated with the same Plates, and he urged the creation of two or three parallel series of figures, "different from the usual ones but satisfying the prerequisites for the individual plates of the basic series" (p. 53).

Rorschach underestimated the difficulty of creating analogous figures, however. Many years of experience have demonstrated that realizing the goal of having Parallel Plates has been somewhat more complicated that it seemed at the time of the publication of *Psychodiagnostics*. During the 1920s the continuing and systematic use of the original series nevertheless contributed to the evolution of the test and also helped to identify the particular characteristics in each of the ten Plates that are most important for purposes of investigation.

What allows the Rorschach to be regarded today as the most valid personality assessment instrument among the projective techniques is the extent to which the basic method proposed by Hermann Rorschach has been supplemented with information from formal and content analyses conducted Plate by Plate. These analyses identify a separate "personality" in each of the Plates with respect to the location choices, determinants, and contents they are likely to generate most often. Once having recognized that interpretations derived from Rorschach protocols are the product of the associations that each of the Inkblots elicit, we can affirm that an efficient series of Parallel Plates will be one that in large part retains the individual personality of each Plate, without altering it completely.

We will turn now to the fundamental concepts that should guide the construction of Parallel Plates, and we will use these concepts as a basis for criticizing previous efforts of this kind. The main point to keep in mind is that each Parallel Plate should include some fundamental characteristics of the original along with some variations that clearly mark it as a unique inkblot in its own right. To begin, then, it is necessary to choose those characteristics of each of the Plates that are really necessary to retain in a Parallel series. As an illustration, the following six features of Plate I can with good reason be considered fundamental characteristics to be retained in a parallel plate:

1. There should be a quality of globality and compactness that fosters whole responses but nevertheless does not prevent detail answers. An appropriate balance must be struck in the frequency with which these two Location choices are likely to occur.

2. The presence of four white details should be retained in a structure in which they are neither too large nor too small. This will allow them to be selected either alone or, as more frequently occurs, in integration with the inked portions of the Plate.

3. The color of the inkblot is important and should comprise different shades of gray-black without being extreme in this regard. Both completely light-shaded or dark-shaded plates should be avoided.

4. The inkblot should allow for numerous popular responses. Ideal in this respect would be an analogous plate on which the whole blot was often seen as one or the other of two popular animals and a detail of the blot also suggested a frequently seen content.

5. The visual impact of the plate in general should contribute to an atmosphere of anxiety and impending difficulty, but it should ordinarily not cause the subject to experience any shock.

6. Aside from seeking a parallel with respect to popular responses, the contents that are elicited by an inkblot are less important than other features of the scoring in seeking to develop an ideal Parallel series. Accordingly, contents will receive relatively less attention in deciding whether a parallel plate will be effective than will be given to the other features of the inkblot.

To date, three series of inkblots have been proposed as Parallel to the Rorschach Plates. These three Parallel series of Plates are known as Be-Ro, Fu-Ro, and Ka-Ro. None of these proposed alternatives to the basic Rorschach has proved entirely adequate.

Rorschach himself collaborated with Behn in 1920 to elaborate the first Parallel Plates. These Plates were published in 1941 by Zulliger in a book devoted to the "Behn-Rorschach Test." The Be-Ro inkblots were sufficiently similar to the original inkblots to confirm expectation that a good parallel series could be developed that would be perceived along the same dimensions as the original series. In relation to paralleling the basic Rorschach, the Be-Ro can be considered relatively satisfactory in many respects. Compared to the original, however, the size is reduced, there are some differences in chromatic coloring, and some stimulus characteristics now recognized as fundamental are not fully matched on a Plate by Plate basis. Hence the Be-Ro cannot be looked upon as an ideal Parallel series.

The second Parallel Series was elaborated in 1938 by Fuchs and published in the United States 20 years later (Drey-Fuchs 1958). Known as the Fu-Ro Test, this is the least parallel of the three series. It is excessively different from the original model, with respect to the general appearance and form of the inkblots and their extremely shaded coloration. The Fu-Ro deviates too far from the basic necessity of preserving structural similarities in devising parallel plates and is therefore likely to differ from the original Rorschach in the structure and symbolism of the responses it evokes. Because of these obvious deficiencies, there has been less work published concerning the Fu-Ro Test than the other two Parallel Series.

The third and most interesting work to date on constructing a Parallel Series has been done by Kataguchi at the Tokyo Institute of Rorschach Research in Japan. Kataguchi developed a series of Plates called the Ka-Ro test in 1963, and 7 years later he published the book *Psychopsy – Manual for Ka-Ro Inkblot Test* (1970). What is especially significant about Kataguchi's work is that his series of Plates are very similar to the basic Rorschach, primarily because they are based on the same principal that has guided our efforts in Rome: namely, to keep the characteristics of the Parallel Plates as similar as possible to those of the original inkblots. However, lack of specific inkblots to match the original prevents us from agreeing with Kataguchi that his work constitutes "the Ideal Parallel Series."

After considering the limitations that have been noted in the three Parallel Series previously in existence, the Scuola Romana Rorschach undertook to develop an entirely new series of Parallel Plates. In this work we have proceeded in a completely different way from the authors before us. Most importantly, we decided to abandon the traditional method of construction used by Hermann Rorschach, in which the final inkblots are chosen from among a great many inkblots that have been produced casually by the technique of dropping ink on a sheet of paper and folding it. We chose instead to produce each inkblot for the new Parallel Series by careful design intended to include on each plate the fundamental characteristics of the original plate for which it would serve as an alternate.

When the proposed design of the new inkblots had been determined, outlines of them were given to two artists. These artists then made as many attempts as possible to duplicate the outlines with the folded paper method. To maintain an "inkblot effect," they folded and pressed together with their fingers pieces of paper with drops of ink on them and chose the best match they could get. Then, following the direction of the authors, they painted in whatever corrections seemed necessary to retain the characteristics of the original Plates. After these corrections were made, the Plates were given to a photographer who produced the actual Plates used in the experiments with this new Parallel Series.

The inkblots that were constructed in this intentional manner were then put to experimental tests, the results of which were used to modify them in whatever ways they appeared not completely to match the originals. The revised blots were then tested experimentally, and further modifications were made in light of the findings. In this way, through three such revisions, the experimental process resulted in four series of Plates, each progressively more correct than its predecessor in meeting the criteria of ideal parallelism to the basic Rorschach.

The final result of this work constitutes the Rorschach Parallel Inkblot Plates proposed by the Scuola Romana Rorschach and published by Parisi and Pes in 1990. It should be noted that the research in developing these parallel Plates was conducted entirely with Italian subjects. For this reason, special attention was called to the possibility of cross-cultural differences during a workshop on the parallel Plates presented in Sao Paolo in 1987. At that time foreign colleagues were invited to begin collecting protocols using the new Parallel Plates, any imperfections of the Plates demonstrated in diverse populations could be addressed by further modifications to produce inkblots specific to those populations.

In each of the experiments with the four series of Plates, the objective was to identify differences between the answers obtained from administering the basic Rorschach Test and from administering one of the Parallel Series. As previously noted, the purpose of these comparisons was to modify the Plates each time, on the basis of the differences identified, to make the final result as similar as possible to the Rorschach test.

The experimentation began with comparison between the Rorschach and Series I of the Parallel Plates in 100 subjects. The differences were so evident that no statistical evaluation was done; instead, a qualitative analysis provide the basis for making the modifications that produced Series II. Subsequently 40 subjects were administered Series II, 32 subjects were administered Series III, and 32 subjects were administered Series IV. Each of the subjects was also administered the basic Rorschach. For each Series, each plate was compared statistically with the corresponding Rorschach Plate, and a detailed analysis was done of the differences between them as reflected in the scores on the Rorschach psychogram. By the time that Series III was reached, the differences from the original Rorschach had been so much reduced that there was no substantial change between Series III and Series IV.

All of the subjects examined in this work were adults between the ages of 20 and 35, equally divided between males and females, who had no history of diagnosed psychopathology or psychotherapeutic treatment and were relatively well educated residents of central Italy. A counterbalanced design was used for administering the tests in each experiment: half of the subjects took the Rorschach first and the Parallel Series second, and the other half took the Parallel Series first. The interval between the two administrations was approximately one month. A brief interview was conducted with each subject prior to the second testing for the purpose of identifying any stressful psychological events that might have occurred in the interval between the two examinations. In each experiment the same examiner administered the procedures in the same environmental conditions, and no indication of the nature of the tests was given to any subject.

Because only limited information was available concerning the background of the subjects, the protocols obtained were not scored for Original (O) and Popular (P) responses, except for scores that were necessary to compete the Neiger Reality Index. Specifically, in evaluating the second, third, and fourth series of Parallel Plates, the following Populars were scored: Plate III, human figure; Plate V, polype or octopus; Plate VIII, four-legged animal; X, any animal, even animals that are not ordinarily scored as Popular on the Rorschach. The variables of the psychogram that were compared statistically for each pair of inkblots in these experiments were the following:

1. Number of responses (R)
2. Number of qualitatively good responses ($R+$)
3. Number of global responses (G)
4. Number of ordinary detail responses (D)
5. Number of good form responses ($F+$)
6. Number of form-color responses (FC)
7. Number of color-form responses (CF)
8. Number of human content responses (H)
9. Number of animal content responses (A)
10. Time to first response (*Reaction Time*)

To take a parametric approach to the data, the inferential statistic used in the analysis was student's *t*. With the exception of *Reaction Time*, however, the variables listed above are expressed in discrete frequencies that are not normally distributed. It was therefore appropriate to work with the squares of these frequencies and thereby promote independence of their mean values and variability. Although the frequency data for these variables could also have been compared using a nonparametric statistical analysis, preference was given to a parametric approach as a means of enhancing the power of the analysis. In those instances in which extremely low frequencies for a variable prevented any reasonable parametric analysis, differences between the Rorschach and the Parallel Plates were determined by examination of median values and frequencies.

I would like to express appreciation to Dr. Fernanado Incurvati, one of the pioneers in the study of the Parallel Plates at the Scuola Romana Rorschach, and Dr. Rosanna Canero Medici, who is responsible for the statistical work at the school, for their contribution to the preparation of this article.

Résumé

Le projet de développer une nouvelle série de taches, parallèle aux planches originales du Rorschach, fut institué pour répondre au besoin, que Rorschach énonça lui-même, de pouvoir administrer le test à un même sujet, à plusieurs reprises et pour des motifs divers (par exemple: visée diagnostique et planification du traitement, recherche longitudinale, études psychopharmacologiques etc. ...). Une série parallèle s'avère particulièrement nécessaire quand la validité du test pourrait être compromise par la connaissance préalable que le sujet aurait acquise des stimuli.

Se distinguant des précédents efforts du genre (Be-Ro en 1941, Fu-Ro en 1958, Ka-Ro en 1970), le projet actuel, commencé en 1974, utilise un procédé expérimental plutôt qu'accidentel pour l'élaboration des taches. Ce procédé crée des taches qui, tout en se différenciant des taches originales par leur apparence, assurent néanmoins – pour chaque planche – la même probabilité d'apparition des diverses Localisations, des Déterminants, des Contenus, des Banalités et autres phénomènes particuliers. Le but consiste à nantir chaque planche parallèle d'un "caractère" particulier, semblable à l'original. Pour y parvenir, les planches parallèles furent progressivement modifiées au cours de trois expérimentations, sur la base des différences émergeant d'une série à l'autre, dans les réponses des sujets.

Plus spécifiquement, des comparaisons statistiques furent établies pour les scores du psychogramme de Rorschach, en utilisant les résultats de sujets ayant passé les deux séries du test. L'ordre de passation fut équilibré, afin qu'une moitié de l'échantillon passe la série originale avant la série parallèle, tandis que l'autre moitié passe les deux séries dans l'ordre inverse. Pour ces derniers, les différences furent analysées à l'aide du "t". Les différences furent analysées à l'aide du "t" pour des groupes corrélés (quand cela était possible) et par des analyses non-paramétriques, pour les variables dont la distribution s'avérait étroite.

Resumen

El proyecto de desarrollar una nueva serie de manchas de tinta, paralela a las láminas originales del Rorschach, se instituyó con el objeto de satisfacer la necesidad, formulada por Rorschach mismo, de administrar el test al mismo sujeto en más de una ocasión o con diferentes propósitos (e. g., diagnóstico y planificación del tratamiento, estudio longitudinal, estudios farmacológicos, etc.). Una serie paralela es particularmente necesaria cuando la validez de la prueba puede ser afectada por la familiaridad previa del sujeto con el estimulo.

A diferencia de los esfuerzos previos de este tipo (Be-Ro en 1941, Fu-Ro en 1958, Ka-Ro en 1970), el presente proyecto, iniciado en 1974, implicó la utilización de un procedimiento experimental para la construcción de las manchas, en lugar de un procedimiento accidental. Este procedimiento crea manchas de tinta que, aunque diferentes en apariencia de las originales, aseguran la correspondencia lámina por lámina, en cuanto a la posibilidad de elicitar ciertas tipos de Localizaciones, Determinantes, Contenidos, Populaces y otros fenómenos especiales. El objetivo consiste en dar a cada lámina paralela un "carácter" particular, similar al de la lámina original. Para lograr este meta, las láminas paralelas fueron progresivamente modificadas durante tres experimentos que permitieron estudiar las diferencias con las láminas originales, en cuanto a como los sujetos respondian a unas y a otras.

Especificamente, se hicieron comparaciones estadísticas para las codificaciones del psicograma del Rorschach usando las láminas originales y paralelas, con grupos de sujetos que respondieron a ambas pruebas. Se balanceó el orden de la administración, de forma que la mitad de los sujetos en cada muestra tomó primero el Rorschach original y luego la serie paralela, mientras que a la otra mitad de los sujetos se les administró las pruebas en el orden inverse. Se analizaron las diferencias con pruebas *t* en la secuencia opuesta. Se analizaron las diferencias con pruebas *t* para grupos correlacionados, cuando resultó apropiado, y con análisis no paramétricos, para variables con una distribución estrecha.

Riassunto

Il progetto di reallizzare una nuova serie di macchie parallele alle Tavole di H. Rorschach risponde all'esigenza, avvertita già dallo stesso Autore, di poter somministrare il reattivo agli stessi soggetti in condizioni e momenti diversi, nei vari ambiti di applicazione (da quello clinico-psicoterapeutico a ricerche di tipo longitudinale, farmacologico, etc.) ed in particolare in quei casi in cui si potrebbe verificare un pre-addestramento del soggetto alla prova (perizie, selezione professionale etc.) che pertanto risulterebbe alterata nella sua validità.

La particolarità di questo lavoro iniziato nel 1974 rispetto ai precedenti tentative (Be-Ro 1941, Fu-Ro 1958, Ka-Ro 1970), consiste nell'aver utilizzato per la costruzione delle macchie una procedura sperimentale, non casuale, basata sulla creazione di serie di macchie che, pur differendo da quelle orininali nelle loro apparenze, potessero garantire tavola per tavola lo stesso equilibrio rispetto al Modo di Comprensione, alle Determinanti, ai Contenuti, alle Frequenze e in taluni casi ai Fenomeni Particolari; tavole quindi che mantenessero quelle stesse caratteristiche che conferiscono a ciascuna tavola Rorschach un particolare "carattere". A tal fine le macchie parallele, dalla serie prototipo a quella definitiva, sono state progressivamente modificate sulla base delle differenze che emergevano tavola per tavola, nelle tre diverse sperimentazioni, dal confronte incrociato con le macchie originali.

Infatti, per verificare l'attendibilità delle nuove macchie sono stati condotti nelle diverse fasi della sperimentazione e per i diverse campioni, confronti statistici e analisi dettagliate delle differenze di rilievo relativamente alle signature fondamentali dello psicogramma Rorschach (R, R+,

G, D, F+, FC, CF, H, A, Lat.). Per casualizzare la veriabile "ordine di somministrazione" è stato effettuato un bilanciamento completo sottoponendo alla prova la metà dei soggetti dei campioni alla sequenza Rorschach-Parallelo, l'altra metà dei soggetti dei campioni alla sequenza inverse.

I risultati ottenuti nelle due prove sono stati quindi confrontati e valutati attraverso il modello probabilistico del t di Student per gruppi correlati e attraverso una analisi delle differenze di rilievo evidenlate dai valori medi e sommatorie delle risposte per quegli indici non confrontabili a livello statistico per il loro esiguo numero.

References

Drey-Fuchs, C. (1958). *Der Fuchs-Rorschach Test*. Göttingen: C. J. Hogrefe.

Kataguchi, Y. (1970). *Psychopsy Manual for the KA-RO Inkblot Test*. Tokyo: Kameko Shobo.

Parisi, S., & Pes, P. (1990). *Tavole Parallele alle Macchie di H. Rorschach (Rorschach Parallel Inkblot Plates)*. Rome: Edizioni Kappa

Rorschach, H. (1921/1942). *Psychodiagnostics*. Bern: Hans Huber.

Zulliger, H. (1941). *Einführung in den Behn-Rorschach-Test*. Bern: Hans Huber.

Gender, Age and Socioeconomic Differences in Rorschach Thematic Content Scales

David Ephraim, Roberta A. Occupati, Juan J. Riquelme, and Elsa C. Gonzalez

Central University of Venezuela

Rorschach content analysis has been and continues to be a very controversial subject. Weiner (1977) has pointed out that Rorschach content interpretations are subjected to error at each step in the inferential process. Lerner (1991) has commented that there is no area of Rorschach analysis more misused and more underused than content. Aronow and Reznikoff (1976) have argued that it will be content interpretation that fulfills the promise of the Rorschach test as a significant and valid assessment instrument. Whatever the importance or limits assigned to content analysis, the different authors agree that Rorschach clinicians rely very much on content in interpreting the test.

Among the nontraditional uses of content indicators (Haley, Draguns, & Phillips, 1967), scales to evaluate psychological variables are again becoming very popular. The type of contents studied, which traditionally have been associated with such variables as anxiety, hostility, or dependency, has recently been extended to include applications of the Rorschach test in studying object relations theories.

Normative and psychosocial considerations combine to warrant the type of research with Rorschach thematic content scales that we report in this paper. On the one hand, progress in research with these variables requires the collection of normative data; there is a notable dearth of normative data bearing content scales (Aronow & Reznikoff, 1976), in contrast to the extensive normative data that are available on Rorschach structural variables (Exner, 1986). On the other hand, we are interested in learning the consequences for Rorschach interpretation, if any, of the postulate that personality is not only resident in the person. It has been claimed that the assumption that persons are self-contained individuals leads to a continued minimization of cultural and subcultural factors in psychological assessment (Dana, 1990).

Taking into account both normative and psychosocial objectives, we have been interested in examining whether psychological aspects of gender, phases in the adult life cycle, and realities of socioeconomic status are differentially reflected in the themes created on the Rorschach test. Research of this kind would contribute to understanding the ever-present interplay between personality and culture (Hallowell, 1953), which can easily be overlooked in clinical use of the instrument. Studies along this line could also reveal whether there are certain response patterns that are normatively associated with gender, age, or socioeconomic level and should not be interpreted as representing some form of individual deviance or psychopathology.

Rorschach contents have been interpreted in relation to numerous aspects of personality functioning, including interests, preoccupations, concerns, underlying conflicts, and self and object representations. The noncritical use of interpretation from the symbolic point of view has been specially troublesome. In our study we will interpret some contents as direct expressions of the individual or group experience (Mayman, 1977). Doing so, we think we shall get closer to what Weiner called a representative interpretation (Lerner, 1991).

Method

Subjects

Protocols from 216 nonpatient adults were collected as part of a Rorschach normative study for the city of Caracas. Subjects were all Venezuelans who had lived in Caracas for a minimum of 10 years and who had no known psychiatric history.

The sample was stratified to obtain groups of equal size foe both sexes (108 subjects each), three age-groups (20–31, 32–43, and 44–55, with 72 subjects each), and four socioeconomic levels (54 subjects each. Socioeconomic status (SES) was evaluated according to a modification of the Graffar Scale (Mendez Castellano & Mendez, 1986); the four SES groups corresponded approximately to upper and upper-middle class (AB), middle class (C), lower class (D), and lower-lower class (E) status. It should be noted that population statistics for Caracas show the following percentages for these groups: AB – 8%; C – 13%; D – 36%; and E – 43%.

Instruments

Rorschach protocols were scored for the following scales and categories: Affective Inferences Scoring System – Revised (Boyer, Dithrich, Harned, Stone, & Walt, 1988); Anxiety and Hostility Scales (Elizur, 1949); Supply: Oral-receptive Orientation (Schafer, 1954); Aggressive Past and Aggressive Potential (Gacono, 1990); Primitive Interpersonal Modes (Kwawer, 1980); Malevolence – Omnipotent Control (derived from Urist, 1977). Information follows on these scales and categories, as well as the reasons that led us to choose them for this study.

The Affective Inferences Scoring System – Revised (AISSR) is a revision and expansion of the Rorschach content category system developed by De Vos (1952). It includes the following content subscales: *anxiety, hostility, dependency, positive, neutral, sexuality,* and *somatization.* The interpretation of some of these scales is problematic as a consequence of their highly inferential psychoanalytic assumptions (e.g., the anxiety subscale includes, among others, fantastic and narcissistic responses). For our study, the AISSR has the advantage of its heuristic potential, derived from the extensive subcategories coverage.

The Elizur *Anxiety* and *Hostility* Scales have been utilized in many studies and have demonstrated that certain aspects of personality can be reliably and validly assessed by thematic Rorschach contents (Aronow & Reznikoff, 1976; Goldfried, Stricker, & Weiner, 1971). Clear definitions and easiness in scoring are some of the advantages of Elizur scales (e.g., responses indicate anxiety if they are characterized by the expression of fear, if the behavior of the percept suggests anxiety, if the response symbolizes anxiety, or if the percept constitutes a cultural stereotype of fear).

Only a few studies have empirically investigated the content themes proposed by Schafer. Of these, most have dealt with the measurement of dependency, particularly the subtheme *supply: oral receptive orientation (Sup)* (Aronow & Reznikoff, 1976).

The subcategories of Gacono, *aggressive past (AgPast)* and *aggressive potential (AgPot)*, make it possible to study aspects of hostility responses that are not specified in such other scales as the *aggressive movement* (AG) of the Comprehensive System (Exner, 1986).

70

The Kwawer scale on *primitive interpersonal modes (Pim)* and his category of *malevolence and omnipotent control (Mal)* constitute new proposals derived from object relations theories. Given that their authors associate this type of responses with severe psychopathology, we considered it particularly interesting to investigate its frequency in a nonpatient group.

Procedure

The Rorschach protocols were administered by 20 clinical psychology students formally trained in the Comprehensive System (Exner, 1990). Most of the examiners were middle class females with a mean age of 24 years. The subjects were volunteers, contacted by the examiners individually and informed that the project concerned standardization of the test. The examiners looked for and tested some subjects of each sex, age, and SES group, using a snow-ball technique. Continuous verifications were made to avoid bias in subject selection.

Due to the validity problem of brief protocols (Exner, 1988), any record containing fewer than 14 answers was discarded. Each Rorschach was scored blindly by two examiners, and

disagreements in scoring were discussed by the research team. Interscorer reliability assessed on a subset of 40 protocols showed a total 93% of agreement.

Results and Discussion

Means were compared to examine differences on the AISSR subscales and Elizur Scales. In no between-group comparison on the Elizur scales were significant differences found. Some significant differences were found on the AISSR subscales, but, because of the heterogeneity of this measure, these differences are difficult to interpret.

Because the distributions for most of the AISSR subcategories and the other themes studied (Sup, AgPast, AgPot, Pim, and Mal) tended to approximate J curves rather than normal curves, groups were compared using a series of chisquares to determine whether the frequencies of subjects giving at least one response of a particular type differed different between groups.

71

In no between-group comparison on *supply: oral receptive orientation* and *malevolence – omnipotent control* were significant differences found. For the *primitive interpersonal modes* scale, an important finding that did emerge was a higher than expected frequency of this type of response in a nonpatient sample: 37.5% of these non-patient subjects gave at least one percept that supposedly represents early stages of levels of relatedness. Some further trends and differences for the AISSR subcategories and other themes are shown in Tables 1, 2, and 3. Comments follow on some of these.

Gender Differences

Examination of Table 1 reveals that women were significantly more likely than men to give protocols containing at least one response from the following subcategories of the AISSR: *internal organs, sexual female anatomy, oral anatomy, childish,* and *rejection and denial.* Men gave significantly more protocols than women in which there were responses from the categories of *explosion, pretentious,* and *science.*

The largest difference between men and women in our samples was a higher frequency of *internal organs* responses in the female group (p .001). Some *internal organs* responses occurred more frequently than others ("lungs" in Cards III, VIII, and X; "stomach" in card III; "kidneys" in Card X), and the great majority of them were minus form quality. There is accordingly reason to suspect that the body preoccupation revealed by these responses is dysfunctional. It is interesting to consider this finding in light of the statement in the *Diagnostic and Statistical Manual of Mental Disorders III-R* (American Psychiatric Association, 1987) that Somatization Disorder is rarely diagnosed in males.

Another gender difference was a greater frequency of protocols with *childish* responses among women than men (e.g., "small elephants together," "teddy bears," "small dolls," "newly born little babies"; the Spanish expressions for these responses are diminutives: "elefanticos," "ositos," "muñequitas," "niñitos recién nacidos"). The subcategories *oral anatomy* and *fusion* also occurred more frequently in the records of women than men. Illustrative *oral anatomy* responses given by our subjects included "face of a person, large mouth," "inner part of a tiger mouth," and "crocodile head with its mouth open."

The interpretation of the higher frequency of these contents in protocols of females remains problematic. Some clinicians consider the use of

72

Table 1. Means, frequencies and chisquare analysis of gender differences on some subcategories of Rorschach Thematic Content Scales.

Subcategory[a]	Women		Men	
	M	Freq.[b]	M	Freq.
Rejection and denial	0.41	29	0.24	17*
Counterphobic	0.35	33	0.28	24
Fantastic	1.24	59	0.93	46
Explosion	0.10	9	0.28	25**
Pretentious	0.12	11	0.39	23*
Sadomasochistic	0.37	25	0.45	35
Anal hostility	0.34	29	0.29	21
Other (hostility)	0.07	6	0.17	16*
Childish	1.07	57	0.59	38**
Oral anatomy	0.56	46	0.43	31*
Fusion	0.67	44	0.45	34
Internal organs	0.86	50	0.36	24***
Sexual female	0.45	32	0.37	20
Body injury	0.19	17	0.32	26
Science	0.22	19	0.41	32*

Note. Only some subcategories on which trends or significant differences were found are included. N = 108 in each subject group.
[a]All subcategories are from the AISSR.
[b]The frequency value indicates the number of individual subjects who produced at least one response in the given category.
*$p < .05$; **$p < .01$; ***$p < .001$.

diminutives as indicative of hysteria. From a less pathological perspective that takes into account gender-role behaviors, the higher frequency of *childish*, *oral anatomy* and *fusion* contents in female protocols could be related to the distinctive focus on nurturance and dependency that accompanies female gender-role socialization. From this perspective we might also be able to explain the minimal interest shown by our female subjects in scientific objects or in technical instruments and procedures (*science* responses).

Men were more likely than women to give aggressive percepts of various types. Also more frequent in the protocols of males were eruptive or explosive activity (*explosion*), intellectual arrogance (*pretentious*), responses that imply a preoccupation with hurting and being hurt (*sadomasochistic*), percepts of body injury or trauma (*injury*), and hostile responses that cannot be scored elsewhere in the AISSR (*hostility – other*).

The tendency shown by our male subjects to give more aggressive contents of these types could be interpreted as reflecting another gender-role behavior: aggression is more socially accepted in men than in women, and the socialization of women emphasizes accommodation and avoidance of conflict.

With respect to the handling of anxiety, the women in our study utilized more than men certain defense mechanisms, such as *rejection and denial* (e. g., the subject denies a previously stated percept) and *counterphobia* (responses that involve attempts to suppress, undo, or otherwise transform threatening, depressive or ugly content: e. g., "Animals fighting? No, they are playing").

Age-Related Differences

Examination of Table 2 reveals that in the first age group a significantly higher number of subjects than in the two older groups gave at least one *fantastic* and one *longing* and/or *security* response; this youngest group was also significantly less likely to give *decorative* responses than the other two groups. The intermediate age group gave a significantly higher number of protocols with *devaluation* than did the other groups and also presented a significantly lower number of protocols with *tension* responses than the youngest group.

Fantastic percepts are most frequent in the protocols of the youngest group. The AISSR includes under this subcategory responses of bizarre, fantastic quality, including contaminations and incongruous combinations of a grotesque and primitive nature. We used a more extensive definition for this subcategory to include inappropriate combinations of any kind (Exner, 1990), and not only the very bizarre ones. In these responses unreal relationships are inferred between images, objects, or activities attributed to objects. The higher frequency of *fantastic* contents of this type in the youngest group suggests that this age group may be described as less reality oriented than the other age groups.

This finding coincides with the results of a previous study with Venezuelan college students, in which a much larger than expected number of inappropriate combination responses was found (Ephraim, Vandroux, & Zárate, 1989).

According to the AISSR, *Longing* responses are those that suggest nostalgia; objects in the distance and reminiscing are included. *Security* percepts are those suggesting a wish for protection and containment, such

Table 2. Means, frequencies and chisquare analysis of age differences on some sub-categories of Rorschach Thematic Content Scales

Subcategory[a]	20–31		32–43		44–55	
	M	Freq.[b]	M	Freq.	M	Freq.
Fantastic	1.31	44	0.99	32[c]	0.96	29[c]
Diffuse	0.86	40	0.68	29	0.61	30
Phallic	1.42	51	1.31	44	0.90	40
Tension	0.44	24	0.17	12[c]	0.43	19
Devaluation	0.19	10	0.39	22[c]	0.43	11[d]
Aggressive past	0.35	18	0.28	16	0.18	9
Nature	0.64	30	0.36	19	0.57	29
Decorative	0.78	31	1.22	46[c]	1.56	48[e]
Longing and /or Security	0.57	26	0.28	11	0.32	15[c]

Note. Only some subcategories on which trends or significant differences were found are included. N = 72 in each subject group.
[a]Except for *Aggressive potential*, the other subcategories are from the AISSR.
[b]The frequency value indicates the number of individual subjects who produced at least one response in the given category.
[c]Significantly different from the first agegroup, $p < .05$.
[d]Significantly different from the second agegroup, $p < .05$.
[e]Significantly different from the first agegroup, $p < .01$.

as houses, castles, caves, and hearths. The lower frequency of protocols with *longing* and/or *security* percepts in those age groups going through more advanced stages of middle adulthood – particularly in the intermediate age group – suggests that at these periods persons are relatively unlikely to grieve for the past or to desire protection, and could thus be described relatively as not being notable dependent.

An interesting but not significant trend was found for *diffuse* responses, which show a slightly elevated frequency in the records of the youngest age group. Diffuse percepts such as clouds, shadows, and smoke suggest diffuse anxiety.

Although not reaching statistical significance at the .05 level, a trend was apparent in the expected direction for *phallic* responses. The youngest group gave a higher frequency of protocols with *phallic* responses than the older groups. Responses in this subcategory include weapons, piercing objects, imaginary figures with phallic attributes, etc. People who produce phallic percepts have been vividly portrayed by Mayman (1984), who relates this type of imagery to a characterological

75

style of meeting competition head on, ever alert to such issues as "Who is ahead?" For this type of person it is particularly important to be strong, or at least to project a strong image in order to ensure that one does not lose the respect of others.

From a developmental perspective all of these differences coincide with intuitive expectations. Younger adults would be expected to be less reality-oriented, more dependent, more anxious, and more concerned with phallic issues than older adults. As might also be expected, older age groups seem more interested than younger people in objects, designs, or ornaments seen as aesthetically attractive (*decoration*).

The intermediate age group gave more protocols than the other groups that contained *devaluation* responses, in which hostility takes the form of depreciation. It is important to note that the examiners considered this age group more difficult to make contact with than the other groups. The lower mean number of responses (R) given by this age group ($M = 19.36$), compared with the youngest ($M = 22.21$) and oldest group ($M = 21.31$), may be related to this issue. That is, the intermediate age subjects could have felt uneasy being tested by younger persons and indirectly expressed their hostility through limiting their responsiveness.

Socioeconomic Level Differences

Examination of Table 3 reveals that in the socioeconomic level (SES) AB group, more subjects gave *paranoid* responses than in the other groups and fewer subjects gave *lifelessness* responses. The majority of the differences with other SES groups reached the .05 significance level.

In the upper SES AB and C groups a significantly higher number of subjects gave *dehumanizing, pretentious*, and *anal anatomy* responses than in the two lower SES D and E groups. A significantly lower number of subjects in the SES E group gave *narcissistic* and *recreation* percepts.

It is not surprising that higher socioeconomic groups gave more positive contents, which involve pleasurable and positive affect; they live in more gentle environments. The major contrast is obviously observed with the SES E group, which gave fewer protocols with responses implying recreational and pleasurable artistic interests, objects, and activities (*recreation*).

These deficits were also observed in the more subjective area of self-perception. The SES E group presented relatively few protocols with *narcissistic* responses. These are percepts involving reflections, twins,

Table 3. Means, frequencies and chisquare analysis of socioeconomic differences on some subcategories of Rorschach Thematic Content Scales.

Subcategory[a]	AB M	Freq.[b]	C M	Freq.	D M	Freq.	E M.	Freq.
Paranoid	1.19	35	0.74	25[c]	0.96	26	0.48	22[c]
Dehumanizing	0.74	31	0.85	31	0.67	22[d]	0.46	21[d]
Narcissism	0.93	28	1.04	29	0.89	30	0.41	15[e]
Pretentious	0.43	15	0.41	12	0.15	06[c]	0.04	02[f]
Ag (Pot)	0.13	06	0.11	06	0.22	10	0.24	13
Cooperative	0.35	18	0.29	15	0.44	23	0.41	18
Recreation	1.33	36	0.98	32	0.96	27	0.52	20
Lifelessness	0.76	24	1.44	39[c]	1.04	34[c]	1.19	32
Anal anatomy	0.33	15	0.17	09	0.11	06	0.11	05[c]

Note. Only some subcategories on which trends or significant differences were found are included. N = 54 in each subject group.
[a]Except for *Aggressive potential*, the other subcategories are from the AISSR.
[b]The frequency value indicates the number of individual subjects who produced at least one response in the given category.
[c]Significantly different from the SES AB, p < .05.
[d]Significantly different from the SES AB and C, p < .05.
[e]Significantly different from all other SES groups, p < .01.
[f]Significantly different from SES AB and C, p < .01.

identical figures, and personal adornments or appearance enhancements that emphasize the body.

Related to the same themes of positive and negative affects and experiences, the data reveal a difference in depressive contents. In this case the higher socioeconomic level group (SES AB) stands apart from the other groups, particularly the middle class (SES C). The *Lifelessness* subcategory, which involves themes of death, decay, loss, aging, and physical deterioration, is responsible for these differences. Perhaps this difference reflects the profound social malaise, experienced particularly by the middle and lower social classes, during recent and unprecedented socioeconomic and political crisis.

A curious finding was a relatively elevated frequency of protocols with *paranoid* responses in the upper and middle-upper social classes (SES AB); the majority of these responses were mask percepts. *Pretentious* and *anal anatomy* responses were also more frequent in this socioeconomic group. The elevated frequency of *dehumanizing* responses in higher and middle social classes (SES AB and C) also merits comment. Although it

77

is difficult to determine what this particular findings might signify, we can at least suggest that having more social and economic resources does not automatically produce more positive interpersonal attitudes. In this regard, we found an just as many or more protocols with *cooperative* responses in the lower social classes (SES D and E) as in the middle and upper classes.

Because of the limitations of the sampling method, the small subgroup size, the numerous comparisons being made, and the uncontrolled effects of the examiners' sex, age and SES, only preliminary conclusions can be drawn from this study. Nevertheless, the findings do appear to identify certain conceptual linkages between the implications of Rorschach thematic contents and aspects of gender socialization, adult developmental phase, and socioeconomic status.

Some of our findings seem to reflect aspects of our particular culture, while others do not. Further studies of this kind with different national or sociocultural groups would be of interest.

Résumé

Dans le cadre de l'interprétation du test de Rorschach, les cliniciens s'appuyent largement sur le contenu des réponses. Pourtant, peu d'information existe quant à l'influence des variables psychosociales sur les contenus au Rorschach, d'où le risque de rendre pathologiques des phénomènes potentiellement normaux. Cette étude examine la nature des différences liées au sexe, à l'âge et au niveau socioéconomique dans la fréquence de réponses au Rorschach, relatives à certaines échelles et catégories de contenus thématiques.

La population de cette étude regroupe 216 adultes nonconsultants, au sein d'un échantillon stratifié, ceci afin d'obtenir des groupes équivalents pour les deux sexes, pour trois groupes d'âge (20–31; 32–43; 44–55) et pour quatre niveaux socio-économiques. Les protocoles furent recueillis dans le cadre d'une recherche normative des variables Rorschach pour la ville de Caracas. Les échelles de contenus utilisées renvoyaient à des variables psychologiques telles que l'anxiété, l'hostilité, la dépendance, la dépression, l'assurance, la somatisation et les modes relationnels primitifs.

Des différences significatives et des tendances marqués émergèrent, notamment dans certaines sous-catégories du Affective Inference Scoring System – Revised (AISS-R). Parmi celles-ci, on trouve chez les femmes, une plus grande fréquence d'*organes internes*, d'*anatomie orale*, de percepts *infantiles*, de *rejet* et de *déni*, tandis que les hommes proposent des contenus d'*explosion*, un savoir *prétentieux* et *scientifique*. En comparaison avec les adultes plus âgés, les jeunes adultes donnent davantage de protocoles avec des percepts *fantastiques*, des réponses liées à la *carence et/ou* à la *sécurite affective* et des contenus *phalliques*. Les sujects avec un niveau socio-économique élevé donnent plus fréquemment des réponse *"masque"* et moins fréquemment des réponses de *dévitalisation* que les sujects d'autres niveaux socio-économiques. Les sujets avec le niveau socio-économique le plus faible donnent moins de réponses *narcissiques* et moins de contenus de *récréation*.

Ces résultats, entre autres, sont interprétés nonsymboliquement, comme des expressions liés à l'expérience de groupe et nous les discutons briévement en termes de socialisation diée au rôle sexué, de problématiques relatives à l'âge et d'événements socio-économiques.

Resumen

Los clinicos se basan mucho en los contenidos al interpretar la prueba de Rorschach. Sin embargo, se sabe poco acerca de la influencia de las variables psicosociales en los contenidos, lo cual puede conducir a considerar como patológicos lo que pueden ser hallazgos normativos. Este estudio investiga las diferencias relacionadas con el género, la subfase del desarrollo adulto y el nivel socioeconómico, en la frecuencia de respuestas en algunas escales y categorias de contenido en el Rorschach.

Los sujetos de este estudio fueron 216 adultos no-pacientes; la muestra fué estratificada con el objeto de obtener grupos equivalentes para ambos sexos, tres niveles de edad (20–31; 32–43: 44–55) y cuatro niveles socioeconómicos. Los protocolos fueron recolectados en el marco de un estudio normativo de variables del Rorschach para la ciudad de Caracas. Las escalas temáticas utilizadas se relacionaban con variables psicológicas tales como ansiedad, hostilidad, dependencia, depresión, afecto positivo, somatización y modalidades primitivas de relación interpersonal.

Se encontraron algunas tendencias y diferencias significativas, particularmente en algunas subcategorias del Sistema de Codificación de Inferencias Afectivas (AISS-R). Entre ellas las siguientes: se presentaron con mayor frecuencia protocolos de mujeres con perceptos de *organos internos, anatomia oral, contenidos infantiles*, y *rechazo y nezación*, mientras que los hombres dieron más protocolos con contenidos de *explosión, pretenciosidad* y *ciencia*. Los adultos más jóvenes dieron más protocolos con contenido *fantastico, fálico* y de *añoranza y/o seguridad* que los adultos de mayor edad. Los sujetos de nivel socio-económico (NSE) alto dieron con mayor frecuencia respuestas de *máscara*, y con menor frecuencia contenidos de *desvitalización*, que los otros niveles socioeconómicos. Los sujetos del NSE más bajo dieron menos protocolos con perceptos de *narcisismo* y *recreación*.

Estos y otros hallazgos son interpretados como expresión de la experiencia del grupo, y discutidos brevemente en términos de la socialización del rol, temas relacionados con la edad y eventos socioeconómicos.

References

American Psychiatric Association (1987). *Diagnostic and statistical manual of mental disorders* (3rd ed. – Revised). Washington DC: American Psychiatric Association.

Aronow, E., & Reznikoff, M. (1976). *Rorschach content interpretation*. New York: Grune and Stratton.

Boyer, L. B., Dithrich, C. W., Harned, H., Stone, J. S., & Walt, A. (1988). *Rorschach handbook for the affective inferences scoring system*. (Available from Boyer Research Institute, 3021 Telegraph Avenue, Suite C, Berkeley, California 94705.)

Dana, R. H. (1990). Crosscultural and multiethnic assessment. In J. N. Butcher & C. D. Spielberger (Eds.), *Advances in personality assessment* (vol. 8; pp. 1–26). Hillsdale, NJ: Lawrence Erlbaum.

Elizur, A. (1949). Content analysis of the Rorschach with regard to anxiety and hostility. *Rorschach Research Exchange and Journal of Projective Techniques, 13*, 247–284.

Ephraim, D., Vandroux, A., & Zárate, Y. (1989). Indices de trastornos del pensamiento en la prueba de Rorschach. Consideraciones teóricas y metodológicas a partir de un estudio comparativo [Rorschach indices of disordered thinking. Theoretical and methodological considerations from a comparative study]. *Psicología, XIV*, 37–48.

Exner, J. E., Jr. (1986). *The Rorschach: A comprehensive system. Vol 1: Basic foundations* (2nd ed.). New York: Wiley.

Exner, J. E., Jr. (1990). *A Rorschach workbook for the comprehensive system* (3rd ed.). Asheville, NC: Rorschach Workshops.

Exner, J. E., Jr. (1991). *The Rorschach: A comprehensive system. Vol 2: Interpretation* (2nd ed.). New York: Wiley.

Gacono, C. (1990). An empirical study of the object relations and defensive operations in antisocial personality disorders. *Journal of Personality Assessment, 54*, 589–600.

Goldfried, M. V., Stricker, G. & Weiner, I. B. (1971). *Rorschach handbook of clinical and research applications.* Englewood Cliffs, NJ: Prentice Hall.

Haley, E. M., Draguns, J. G., & Phillips, L. (1967). Studies of Rorschach content: a review of research literature. Part II: Nontraditional uses of content indicators. *Journal of Personality Assessment, 31*, 3–37.

Hallowell, I. (1953). The Rorschach technique in personality and culture studies. In B. Klopfer, M. D. Ainsworth, W. G. Klopfer, & R. Holt (Eds.), *Developments in the Rorschach technique* (Vol. II). New York: Harcourt, Brace & World.

Kwawer, J. S. (1980). Primitive interpersonal modes, borderline phenomena and Rorschach content. In J. S. Kwawer, H. D. Lerner, & P. M. Lerner (Eds.), *Borderline phenomena and the Rorschach Test.* New York: International Universities Press.

Lerner, P. M. (1991). The analysis of content revisited. *Journal of Personality Assessment, 56*, 145–157.

Mayman, M. (1977). A multidimensional view of the Rorschach movement response. In M. A. Rickers-ovsiankina (Ed.), *Rorschach psychology* (2nd ed. pp. 229 – 250). Huntington, New York: Krieger.

Mayman, M. (1984, July). *Rorschach imagery: Reflections of an inner object world.* Paper presented at the XI International Congress of Rorschach and other Projective Techniques. Barcelona, Spain.

Mendez Castellano, H., & Mendez C. (1986). Estratificación social y biología humana [Social stratification and human biology]. *Archivos Venezolanos de Puericultura y Pediatría, 49*(3 y 4), 93–104.

Schafer, R. (1954). *Psychoanalytic interpretation in Rorschach testing.* New York: Grune & Stratton.

Urist, J. (1977). The Rorschach test and the assessment of object relations. *Journal of Personality Assessment, 41*, 3–9.

Weiner, I. B. (1977). Approaches to Rorschach validation. In M. A. Rickers-ovsiankina (Ed.), *Rorschach psychology* (2nd ed.; pp. 575–608). Huntington, NY: Krieger.

Author Notes

This article was based on a study supported in part by the Consejo de Desarrollo Científico y Humanístico, Universidad Central de Venezuela. We gratefully acknowledge the contributions of Giovanna Pavan, Luis Garmendia, Catrin Ramirez, Carmen Maria Ivashevski and Debora Urribarri in the data collection.

The Thematic Rorschach: A Proposal for the Clinical Evaluation of the Rorschach Responses

Andre Jacquemin and M. Iozzi

University of Sao Paolo, Ribeirao, Sao Paolo, Brazil

The objective of the present paper is to describe a new procedure that extends the exploration of Rorschach responses in order to enrich their interpretation. Described by Draime (1973) in a study on the symbolic value of Card IV, this technique, called "The Thematic Rorschach," fills some interpretive gaps that usually exist when responses to the test are explored only in the traditional manner. Indeed, unexplored responses often yield minimal information and fail to show much relationship with one another.

The idea of expanding the information obtained about the content of Rorschach responses is not new. Different studies have suggested the use of free-association techniques for this purpose. We may cite the studies by Elizur (1976), Aronow and Reznikoff (1979), Edington (1980), and De Tichey and Lichezzolo (1983), whose results have pointed out the richness of the procedure with respect to providing significant clinical data for a dynamic understanding of personality. When used in the form reported in the above studies, however, the free-association technique is quite limited because it focuses on each response separately. This focus on responses separately prevents the capturing of possible relations existing among responses and the possible surfacing of expressive elements of the affective life of the individuals tested. Within this context, the procedure proposed here is original in terms of inducing an articulation of the responses given by an individual, as determined during a second phase of inquiry after the traditional administration of the test. For each card, the subject is asked to tell a story that integrates all of the responses given to that card, and these stories embellish even static contents with dynamic aspects.

Accordingly, the present study expands the approach of Rorschach (1942), who originally placed primary emphasis on the perceptive aspects of this technique. Indeed, in his *Psychodiagnostics: A Diagnostic Test Based on Perception*, Rorschach clearly revealed his perceptive approach to what is produced by individuals:

> "The interpretation of the chance forms falls in the field of perception and apperception rather than imagination" (p. 16).
>
> "There is, therefore, no doubt that this experiment can be called a test of the perceptive power of the subject" (p. 18).

Although Rorschach was originally seeking a technique for evaluating psychic functioning through examining perceptual processes, i. e., processes based on the form of apperception of immediate reality, later studies have expanded his focus without entirely discarding his assumptions. Recently, Rausch de Traubenberg (1983) advanced the hypothesis that the Rorschach test may correspond to a space of interaction between perceptive and phantasmic activity, between the external reality of the known object and the internal reality of the experienced object. When these elements are considered, the Thematic Rorschach offers new possibilities for investigating the interrelationship between what is real and what is imagined. Whereas the traditional application of the test tends to reach the perceptive level, especially in normal subjects, the elaboration of stories can reach the phantasmic level.

The present study sought to determine the usefulness and viability of the "Thematic Rorschach" as a complementary technique in efforts to understand personality and the personality of children in particular. Socioeconomically underprivileged children were selected as subjects for this study because they represent a large part of the Brazilian population. An attempt was also made to determine the influence of different levels of deprivation on the productivity of the children, especially in their stories.

Methodology

Sample

The study was conducted on 30 children of both sexes aged 9 to 11 years and of low socioeconomic level. The children were divided into two groups: Group A (n = 20) were attending school on a regular basis and receiving adequate nutrition; Group B (n = 10) were attending school irregularly, were not at expected grade level for their age, and generally were living in more precarious circumstances with greater real material and emotional deprivation than Group A.

Procedure

The Rorschach cards were used in two phases of examination in a single experimental session with each child. The first phase involved traditional administration of the Rorschach test, including a complete inquiry as recommended by Beizmann (1961) and Jacquemin (1977). In the second phase, following a short interval for rest, the children were asked to imagine a story that would include all of the answers they had given to each stimulus during the traditional administration of the test. In this thematic phase, the blots are presented again one by one together with a card containing the responses to each blot. The following instructions are read aloud:

> "I will show you again the ten pictures I already presented to you. Here are the replies you gave me. I would like you to tell me a story for each picture, using all the replies you gave me. Now, in this picture you saw 'x,' 'y,' and 'z.' So, tell me a story about 'x,' 'y,' and 'z.' "

In practically all cases, the children in this research reacted positively to these instructions and were able to perform the task satisfactorily.

Results

Because the major objective of this research was to determine the extent to which the proposed Thematic Rorschach procedure is viable and revealing in work with children, the results of the traditional administration of the Rorschach – the psychogram – will not be presented. With regard to stories given in response to the thematic procedure, these were analyzed according to the list of needs used with Murray's (1951) Thematic Apperception Test, as recommended by Ombredane (1969) and Morval (1962). In addition to providing a means of objectifying the stories, analyzing the configuration of needs represented in them permits "a dynamic evaluation of personality, since it demonstrates what the motor element of behavior consists of" (Morval, 1982, p. 31). Along with reporting these data, some actual stories of the children will be presented and briefly analyzed to illustrate the richness and significance of children's productions generated by this method.

Analysis of Needs

Table 1 presents the percentages of the needs most frequently encountered in the stories imagined by the children in each of the two groups studied. It can be seen that more than 40% of the needs encountered in the two groups are characterized by aggression and destruction. These apparent preoccupations reveal that the underprivileged children studied here are marked by impulses of a primitive type, with reduced control. Not even the better living conditions of Group A (who were receiving more attention and support in their environment than Group B) seem sufficient to reduce this intense manifestation of aggressiveness. All of the children tested are from a disadvantaged social class seriously lacking in resources, although Group A children experience less severe deprivation than Group B children. Their families are usually very large and live in crowded slum neighborhoods in which impulsive aggressive and sexual behaviors can frequently be observed. Poverty and poor living conditions are prominent characteristics of their life experience.

Thus, it may be that these real deprivations, with a consequent daily experience of frustration, combine with deprivation at the phantasmic

Table 1. Needs observed in the Thematic Rorschachs of two groups of underprivileged children (in percentages).

Needs	Group A (N = 20)	Group B (N = 20)
Aggression – destruction	43.0	42.0
Affiliation – reclaimed protection	14.0	23.0
Protection – exerted	6.0	2.0
Realization – Self-appreciation	5.0	3.0
Acquisition	6.5	0.0
Alimentation	5.5	3.0
Amusement	5.5	10.0
Other needs	6.0	7.0
Absence of stories	8.5	10.5
	100.0	100.5

level to stimulate the high frequency of aggressive and destructive themes found in the stories told by the children. The impulsiveness suggested by their stories may dispose these children to behave aggressively, perhaps as a consequence of models of aggressive interaction observed in their family environment. However, it is also possible that these children may experience their aggressiveness in a latent form not directly manifested in behavioral activities but only as a subliminal element of their affectivity, and possibly surfacing at unexpected times in the form of "aggressive explosions." Further investigation of these alternative possibilities will require extensive longitudinal follow-up of individual cases, which is beyond the scope of the present study.

In a study of children's production of stories to inkblots they created themselves, Edington (1980) also observed intensely violent fantasies representative of emotional needs in children who were underprivileged. This author reported further that direct expressions of personal dissatisfaction in the form of stories with aggressive content tended to diminish over time as these children were treated in ongoing psychotherapy. These findings, taken together with our own results, lead us to think that the stories told by these children do indeed contain emotional indicators of the high level of real frustrations they experience. Their verbal productions tend to reflect fairly directly the underlying impulsiveness associated with their having so few environmental resources for meeting their personal needs. However, when they receive some type of satisfaction, as in psychotherapy, these children may become less inclined toward direct expression of their aggressiveness, perhaps by internalizing other models with whom they have formed a relationship.

To continue the analysis of the needs that were most frequently detected in the stories told by our subjects, note that the frequency of "affiliation" and "reclaimed protection" was substantially higher in the more underprivileged group (Group B). Group B children thus showed a greater need for support, understanding, and affiliation than was manifested by Group A children, who are routinely more protected. This suggests the hypothesis that children who are indeed more deprived clearly indicate their greater dissatisfaction at the affective level, by more strongly requesting protective action on the part of the environment. These more deprived children reveal feelings of insecurity and personal fragility that are more intense than those of children who still receive a minimum of external support. Thus, the harmful interference of severe and continuous privations with the development of children's personality is clearly demonstrated.

On the other hand, Group A showed greater needs than Group B for achievement, self-appreciation, and activities involving the exercise of protection, which indicates the desire of these children to concretize personal projects in an active form. This active orientation tends to differentiate these children from the more underprivileged ones; Group B children are characterized by needs of a passive type (receiving help and affection), whereas Group A children show signs of initiative and the ability to produce. In contrast to the more prominent needs for achievement observed in Group A children, the more underprivileged children in Group B display more prominent needs for "amusement." This suggests to us that Group A children, by having some of their basic needs satisfied, seem to feel more secure and better capable of interacting with the environment in an active manner, looking for personal fulfillment. The more underprivileged children in Group B, on the other hand, seem to view themselves as more fragile and less able and to seek satisfaction in a compensatory manner at the amusement level and perhaps with regressive ways of reacting, to alleviate their daily frustrations.

Also very interesting is the difference between the two groups in the frequency of their needs for "acquisition" and "alimentation." These needs tend to be more prominent in group A than in group B. Perhaps the prospects of obtaining material objects in a concrete manner is so remote for seriously underprivileged children that it becomes of little importance in stimulating or motivating capacity in their behavior. These children seem to see themselves as so markedly limited in possibilities for obtaining nurturance or material satisfaction that they focus their attention on other alternatives, either at the affective or at the amusement level, that usually do not depend on the kinds of material subsidies that are so scarce in the lives of these children.

Group A children, on the other hand, tend to experience less depriving living conditions and to encounter more situations in which needs for achievement, for exerting an active impact on the environment, and for alimentation and acquisition are in some way satisfied. Hence, these needs persist as stimulating and motivating characteristics for these children, in contrast to the even less privileged group. No other differences in thematically expressed needs were observed in the stories of these two groups of children.

Analysis of Themes

Having examined the types of needs detected in the children's productions using this new technique, we shall now turn to other indications of the richness of the material that can be collected using the Thematic Rorschach test procedure. As noted earlier, responses to the traditionally administered Rorschach test do not reveal explicitly the particular meanings of percepts, which limits possibilities for analyzing the phantasmic level underlying the contents. When the new technique is used, a simple "butterfly" response given by three different children as their only answer to Card V reflects affective and phantasmic experiences of the children that can be explored in a very revealing manner through stories elaborated about it. As illustrations, consider the following stories:

> Subject A: a 10-year-old boy
> "Once upon a time, a butterfly wanted to go to the swamp. When it arrived there, it saw many beautiful animals. Except that it found the alligator ugly. One day, when the butterfly went to sleep, it rested on the alligator's head. Then, the alligator woke up and ate the butterfly. That's all."

> Subject B: a 10-year-old girl
> "A butterfly flew into the forest and then came back. In the field the butterfly died because it got tired of flying. I don't know anything else."

> Subject C: a 10-year-old girl
> "Once upon a time there was a very ugly butterfly. The butterfly was very sad because all the others were beautiful. Then the butterfly met a turtle and the turtle was very ugly. Then the butterfly and the turtle lived happily ever after."

The structure of the "butterfly" response – Gp F+ A Ban – contains very few idiographic or personal elements for analysis and constitutes simply a "banal" or "popular" apperception of the stimulus. Although a well-adapted apperception indicating apparently adequate personality organization, it provides little information about underlying thoughts and feelings.

However, analysis of the stories told about this banal response reveals some fairly obvious personal characteristics suggested by the particular way in which each child elaborated the plot of the story. Thus, Subject A clearly expressed concerns about aggressive relationships between living things, suggesting that he may perceive interpersonal contacts as threatening. The story imagined by the second child is quite different in that the "not knowing" appears to signal a more fragile identity. As a further difference, the butterfly in the story by Subject B ends up by devitalizing itself due to its own tiredness, through a personal act (perhaps a self-destructive one), but without the involvement of an aggressive external element. Subject C showed more formal richness in her story than the other two children, by structuring it with elements of the present and the future. Although she initially expressed a negative self-image ("ugly"), she seemed able to use contact with reality (there also are others who are "ugly") as a basis for elaborating her perception into a stimulus and environmental support for continuing her life.

These brief comments on stories produced by children about their responses to the Rorschach test should suffice to demonstrate how analysis of the personal meanings attributed to percepts can clarify and enrich our understanding of the emotional experience of subjects being evaluated.

Conclusion

In view of the above considerations, we believe that the "Thematic Rorschach" is a useful and generative technique for obtaining information about the dynamics of personality functioning with which to complement what may be learned from the data in the traditional psychogram.

Although further research is needed to systematize this technique and to evaluate its clinical validity, the present study demonstrates the interpretative breadth that can be achieved by this complementary form of response investigation. It is not our intention to use this innovation as a substitute for other thematic tests, such as the CAT. Rather, this is a procedure for obtaining additional valuable information in the clinical interpretation of the Rorschach test itself.

In applying the Thematic Rorschach procedure, clinicians need to take care to avoid personalized or biased analyses of the percepts. Errors of interpretation commonly occur when symbols are assumed because of personal belief or bias to have some single, unvarying, or universal meaning, without considering the particular living experience of the individual. As pointed out by Edington (1980), it is unwise to construct symbolic interpretative hypotheses without sufficient confirmatory data, because doing so may result in mistaken inferences that have no meaning for the characteristics of the individual in question. Thus, the informative complement provided by associations made after the responses is useful, as proposed by the "Thematic Rorschach."

Although proceeding with the different objective of looking for a strictly psychoanalytic analysis of free associations, De Tichey and Lichezzolo (1983) have also pointed out how this type of procedure can enhance the analysis of Rorschach protocols without in any way neglecting the original purpose and approach of the test's author. They stress that the two approaches relate to each other in a complementary and not a competitive fashion. In their view, the two approaches measure different levels of the functioning of personality, with the classic procedure being more focused on the structural organization of the subject and the associative technique emphasizing the present and past dynamics that have determined this organization.

In this presentation we have demonstrated the potential value of using the "Thematic Rorschach" in the clinical evaluation of personality, especially with children, which was the objective of our study.

Résumé

Cette étude avait pour objectif d'évaluer l'utilité et la viabilité de la technique du "Rorschach thématique", laquelle consiste à demander au sujet de raconter une histoire à partir de ses réponses au test.

Trente enfants des deux sexes, âgés de 9 à 11 ans, et de faible niveau socio-économique, furent étudiés. Les enfants furent répartis en deux groupes: le groupe A (N = 20) présente une scolarité régulière et une bonne alimentation, tandis que le groupe B (N = 10) présente une scolarité irrégulière et des conditions de vie, dans l'ensemble, défavorisées.

Les histoires racontées furent évaluées cliniquement, à l'aide de la liste des besoins de MURRAY, démontrant ainsi la richesse interprétative d'une procédure, susceptible de venir compléter l'application traditionnelle du test.

Andre Jacquemin and M. Iozzi

Resumen

El objetivo de la presente investigación fué determinar la utilidad y viabilidad de la técnica del "Rorschach Temático", la cual consiste en invitar al sujeto a contar una historia usando sus propias respuestas a la prueba.

Se estudiaron treinta niños de ambos sexos, con edades comprendidas entre los 9 y los 11 años, y de un nivel socioeconómico bajo. Los niños se dividieron en dos grupos: los del Grupo A (N = 20) asistian regularmente al colegio y recibian buena alimentación. Los del Grupo B (N = 10) asistian irregularmente al colegio y vivian bajo condiciones generales de deprivación.

Las historias obtenidas fueron evaluadas clinicamente y de acuerdo a la lista de necesidades de Murray, y mostraron la amplitud interpretativa que puede ser lograda a través de este procedimiento, como complemento a la aplicación tradicional del test.

Resumo

A presente investigacão teve como objetivo verificar a utilidade e viabilidade da técnica do "Rorschach Temàtico" que consiste em convidar o sujeito a contar uma estòria, utilizando-se de suas próprias respostas.

Trinta criancas de ambos os sexos, na faixa etária de 09 and 11 anos e com nível sócio-ecnômico baixo, foram estudadas. Dois grupos foram avaliados: o grupo A (N = 20) com escolaridade regular e boa alimentacão; o grupo B (N = 10) com escolaridade irregular e condicões gerais de vida sofrida.

As estórias obtidas foram avaliadas de maneira clínica e de acordo com a lista das necessidades de Murray, mostrando a amplitude interpretativa que pode ser alcancada através deste procedimento complementar à aplicacão tradicional.

References

Aronow, E., Reznikoff, M., & Rauchway, A. (1970). Some old and new directions in Rorschach testing. *Journal of Personality Assessment, 43*, 227–234.

91

Beizmann, C. (1961). Le Rorschach chez l'enfant de 3 à 10 ans. In Neuchatel (Ed.), *Delachaux & Niestlé*.

De Tichey, C., & Lighezzolo, J. (1983). A propos de la dépression "limite": Contribution du test de Rorschach em passation "classique" et "psychanalytique." *Psychologie Francaise, 28*, 141–156.

Draime, J. (1973). *La spécificité de la plache IV du test de Rorschach-approche expérimentale*. Mémoire Inédit. Université Catholique de Louvain, Faculté de Psychologie et des Sciences de l'Education.

Edington, G. E. (1980). An ink-blot story technique with children, preliminary observations. *Perceptual and Motor Skills, 51*, 283–286.

Elizur, B. (1976). Content analysis of the Rorschach in two phases: Imaginary story and self-interpretation. *Perceptual and Motor Skills, 43*, 43–46.

Iozzi, M., & Jacquemin, A. (1987). O Rorschach-Temático: uma exploracão da Prancha V. *Rorschachiana, XVI*, 276.

Jacquemin, A. (1977). *O teste de Rorschach em criancas brasileiras: Pesquisa e atlas*. São Paulo, Vetor, 1977.

Morval, M. V. G. (1982). *Le TAT at les fonctions du moi*. 2a. ed. Montréal: Presses de l'Université de Montréal.

Murray, H. A. (1951). *Teste de apercepcion temática*. Buenos Aires: Ed. Paidós.

Ombredane, A. (1969). *L'exploration de la mentalité des noirs*. Paris: Presses Universitaires de France.

Rausch de Traubenberg, N. (1983). Actividade perceptiva e actividade fantasmática no teste de Rorschach. O Rorschach: espaco de interacões. *Análise Psicológica, 4*, 17–22.

Rorschach, H. (1942). *Psicodiagnostics*. 2a. ed. Trad. Inglesa, Berne: Verlag Hans Huber.

Contemporary Trends in Rorschach Research in Japan

Toshiki Ogawa

University of Tsukuba, Japan

The Rorschach test has a long history in Japan. Merely 4 years after the publication of *Psychodiagnostics*, Japanese psychologist and psychiatrists took a keen interest in this test. The major advances in Rorschach research in Japan occurred after World War II, however, these developments coincided with the growth of clinical psychology in Japan. Professor Kataguchi (1957) has summarized these historical developments in detail. The present paper discusses the contemporary status of Rorschach research in Japan (1980–1990). The current status in Japan of the Rorschach test as a clinical instrument is considered first, after which the leading Rorschach studies that have been undertaken in this country during the past decade are reviewed.

Rorschach Test Usage in Japan

In Japan as in many other countries, various psychological tests are used in clinical practice. What status does the Rorschach test have as a clinical instrument in Japan, and how do Japanese clinical psychologists evaluate this test?

Ogawa and Piotrowski (1992) surveyed members of the AJCP (Association of Japanese Clinical Psychology) regarding the psychological tests used in their practice. As Table 1 indicates, the Rorschach was the most frequently used test, followed in order by the SCT, Baumtest, and WAIS. When asked which tests are indispensable for their daily practice, about one-third of the respondents designated the Rorschach. When these AJCP members were asked which tests they deemed essential to the competent clinical practice, the Rorschach ranked at the top of the

93

Table 1

Table 1. Frequency of usage of various psychological tests in Japan (Ogawa & Piotrowski, 1992).

Test	Never	Occasionally	Moderately	Frequently	Always	Rank
Rorschach	16 (14%)	18 (15%)	30 (26%)	21 (18%)	31 (27%)	1
S.C.T.	14 (12%)	25 (21%)	43 (37%)	21 (18%)	13 (11%)	2
Baumtest	21 (18%)	23 (20%)	26 (22%)	25 (21%)	21 (18%)	3
WAIS	23 (20%)	21 (18%)	43 (37%)	15 (13%)	9 (8%)	4
Binet	22 (19%)	24 (21%)	42 (36%)	15 (13%)	9 (8%)	5
Yatabe-Guilford	23 (20%)	33 (28%)	35 (30%)	13 (11%)	11 (9%)	6
WISC-R	37 (32%)	23 (20%)	39 (33%)	10 (9%)	5 (4%)	7
House-Tree-Person	35 (30%)	26 (22%)	29 (25%)	13 (11%)	11 (9%)	8
P-F Study	32 (27%)	33 (28%)	33 (28%)	14 (12%)	3 (3%)	9
Bender-Gestalt	26 (22%)	44 (38%)	30 (26%)	11 (9%)	4 (3%)	10
Utida-Kraepelin	37 (32%)	32 (27%)	31 (27%)	10 (9%)	3 (3%)	11
Draw-A-Person	47 (40%)	26 (22%)	26 (22%)	9 (8%)	6 (5%)	12
Family Drawing	49 (42%)	30 (26%)	24 (21%)	6 (5%)	5 (4%)	13

Note: Rank as calculated by summing the three usage ratings of moderately, frequently, and always.

list, with the WAIS ranked second. Thus, it is clear that the Rorschach is an essential tool of clinical psychologists in Japan.

Contemporary Rorschach test procedures have evolved from several different theoretical approaches. As a result, various scoring systems are in use. Table 2 shows the scoring systems that are utilized by clinicians in Japan, ranked according to the frequency of their use in daily clinical practice.

Table 2. Percentage of respondents who indicated their scoring systems used in practice.

Scoring system	Percentage
Kataguchi	78.7
Osaka University	10.7
Nagoya University	9.3
Others	1.3

Table 3. Proportion of respondents' preference for foreign scoring systems.

Scoring system	Percentage
Klopfer	74.7
Beck	9.7
Rapaport & Schafer	8.8
Piotrowski	4.9
Exner	2.0

The Kataguchi and Osaka University scoring systems are both essentially modifications of the Klopfer system. The Nagoya University scoring system is based on the Beck system and has in addition adapted DeVos affective symbolism. Overall, Kataguchi's system ranks first, with 78.7% of the respondents indicating that they use it. The Osaka University and the Nagoya University systems are preferred in their respective local areas.

Table 3 indicates the theoretical influence of non-Japanese Rorschach scholars in this country. Since Kataguchi's very popular scoring system is based mainly on Klopfer's method, Klopfer is the best known non-Japanese Rorschach scholar in Japan.

Klopfer's manual *The Rorschach Technique*, Beck's book *The Rorschach Test: Exemplified in Classics of Drama and Fiction*, and Piotrowski's textbook *Perceptanalysis* have been translated into Japanese at the time of this survey. Thus, Japanese clinical psychologists are familiar with the ideas of these scholars. In addition, as theoretical references, the following books were introduced to Japan before 1980: Schachtel's *Experiential Foundations of Rorschach's Test*; Weiner's *Psychodiagnosis in Schizophrenia*; Exner's *The Rorschach Systems*; and McCully's *Rorschach Theory and Symbolism*. Most recently, a Japanese version of Exner's *The Rorschach: A Comprehensive System* was published. Therefore, clinical psychologists in

95

Japan have had an opportunity to become well-informed about this broad subject.

Rorschach Research from 1980–1990

Although at present there is no official Rorschach society in Japan, a specialized journal, *Rorschachiana Japonica*, is issued annually. This journal was first published in 1958 under the leadership of Professor Kataguchi. It was intended to promote active interchange among Rorschach workers in Japan, much as did the Rorschach Research Exchange in the United States. In addition to appearing in this journal, research on the Rorschach test is also published in the official journals of psychological and medical associations. Because a great many Rorschach studies are reported every year in Japan, the present paper will summarize only the most important Japanese research undertaken during the last decade.

In Japan, during these 10 years, there has been an increase in the number of clinical studies published and a decrease in the number of basic experimental studies. For example, research using the tachistoscopic and semantic differential methods, which was widespread during the 1960s, is rarely reported now, except for a few experimental studies using an ophthalmograph (Tanaka et al., 1980; Harada et al., 1982). Borderline personality disorders, eating disorders, and family therapy are particularly noteworthy among subjects of Rorschach research at the present time.

Studies on Schizophrenia

There has been enormous attention to schizophrenia in Japanese Rorschach studies. Hermann Rorschach himself pointed out how much the test can contribute to the differential diagnosis of schizophrenia, and there is accordingly nothing surprising in how many Rorschach studies focus on the psychopathology of schizophrenic disorders. Even so, the volume of Rorschach research concerned with the diagnosis and treatment of schizophrenics that has been undertaken during these 10 years in Japan is truly impressive.

Hirose and Nomura (1981) investigated the relationship between changes in Rorschach responses and the social adjustment of chronic schizophrenics. They retested 13 patients 7 to 11 years after their initial examination. They found that poor social re-adjustment was more likely to be associated with emotional constriction and poor will than with emotional instability, weak reality testing, or limited self-control. Specifically, the presence of rejections, a large number of popular responses, a small number of content categories, and a high percentage of DeVos' neutral response appeared to be signs of poor prognosis.

Sorai (1982) administered the Rorschach individually to 50 schizophrenic inpatients at admission to the hospital and retested them at discharge. So-called failure patients, who were re-hospitalized within one year, were likely to have shown a decrease in FM responses between the two testings, an increase in Cds response, and a high F%. As for patients who succeeded in maintaining an adequate level of social adjustment for 6 or 7 years, their records were notable for a variety of determinant characteristics. The most striking of these was a change in the modified BRS (Basic Rorschach Score). The author concluded that the success group showed more improvement in personality integration than the failure group, as indicated by a positive sift of more than nine points on the modified BRS.

Shibata and and her colleagues also investigated the prognosis of schizophrenics by means of the modified BRS (Shibata, et al., 1987; Takahashi, et al., 1987). They found that a score of −10 on the modified BRS was a critical value. Schizophrenic female inpatients whose modified BRS never exceeded -10 were never re-hospitalized after discharge. The authors also found that both R+% and D/D+W% were good predictive indices. A D/D+W% of more than 40% and an R+% from 45 to 50 were associated with readjusting well to society. These findings were confirmed in a further study by these authors in which 40 schizophrenic male patients participated; however, in this further sample the results were not always found for paranoid schizophrenics.

Recently, Unai and Kato (1988) examined the correspondence between a clinical evaluation of prognosis and Piotrowski's Prognostic Index. This index consists of two subcategories: a short-term prognostic index and a long-term prognostic index for 3 to 6 years. They found a close relationship between clinical estimates of prognosis at discharge and the short-term prognostic index. A value of +2 on the index appeared to be an effective cut-off point for predicting favorable social adjustment.

Taken together, these findings based on the Rorschach test have significant implications for the psychotherapy of schizophrenia and even more so for the rehabilitation of schizophrenic patients. Clearly the Rorschach is a powerful tool for differential diagnosis as well as for prognostic estimation.

Research on Eating Disorders

In Japan, anorexia nervosa was a central concern in psychiatry and psychosomatic medicine during the 1970s. Subsequently, many Rorschach studies on anorexia nervosa were reported in the 1980s.

Akitani (1981) found the following features among young girls diagnosed as anorexic: delayed response time of first response, the presence of achromatic responses on Card I, dominance of W responses, an emotional pattern of CFFC, more (H) responses than H responses, and appropriate form quality.

Tohyama (1983) compared the Rorschach protocols of juvenile anorexic patients with those of normal subjects. These two groups differed significantly in such variables as R, W%, Dd%, FC, DR, CR, and F+%. In particular, the anorexics gave fewer responses, a higher W%, a lower Dd% and F+%, fewer FC, and less variety of determinants and contents. It was accordingly inferred that the anorexic patients tended to suppress and thus suffer a decrease in mental productivity in spite of maintaining an appropriate level of intelligence. Tohyama suggested that a passive submissive attitude, overcontrol of emotional expression, and defective behavioral control are basic personality characteristics of anorexics.

Some researchers have attempted to classify anorexia nervosa into subcategories. Nadaoka et al. (1980) investigated two groups of anorexic patients, a typical group that met Feighner's diagnostic criteria for anorexia nervosa, and an atypical group that only partially met the criteria. The Rorschachs of the typical group were low both on the modified BRS and in RPRS. This typical group cold be differentiated further into two subgroups. One subgroup appeared less sympathetic and more stereotyped, showed less R and M, had a high W% and A%, and was coartative. The other subgroup was characterized by inner conflicts that were reflected in more R and M, a high W%, and a low R+%.

Applying concepts of Palazzoli, Oka et al. (1985) used the Rorschach to discriminate a stable type of anorexia nervosa from an unstable type.

Compared to normal expectation, the stable anorexics gave fewer responses, a high W%, a low Dd%, and fewer chromatic color responses. The records of the unstable type were characterized by the presence of anatomy or blood responses and by more frequent M than FM responses. Oka et al. interpreted their findings to mean that the pathological level of anorexia nervosa is more severe than the neurotic level, and they concluded that overcontrol, both by inner inhibitory self-punishment and by outer overadaptiveness, is very salient in anorexics.

Shimada et al. (1985) sought to clarify the nature of eating disorders by means of the Rorschach. They classified eating disorder patients into four groups on the basis of their Experience Balance. They found that the Experience Balance of anorexics was introversive, whereas in bulimics it was extratensive, coartative, or ambiequal.

Thus, many consistent findings have emerged from Rorschach studies of anorexia nervosa (e. g. a high frequency of M and a low frequency of chromatic color response). However, there are some persistent methodological problems in this area of research. Eating disorders are contemporary psychological disturbances that are very much in fashion. As a result, they have become defined in an increasingly broad manner. Future Rorschach studies on anorexia nervosa and bulimia nervosa will benefit from more precise diagnostic criteria for eating disorders than have been in use.

Other Clinical Research

Rorschach workers, who tend to be dynamically oriented in their approach to psychology, generally pay little attention to neurological disease. Nevertheless, several articles concerning Rorschach assessment in neurological disturbance have been published in Japan.

Aoki and Kawai (1982) examined Rorschach differences between the awake type of epilepsy and the sleep type of epilepsy. They found that reality testing was weak in the awake type and that these epileptics gave numerous chromatic color and texture responses. In the sleep type of epilepsy, reaction time was slow, and these epileptics gave numerous animal responses and many pure form responses. These findings indicate that sleep type epileptics are likely to be active and assertive, whereas awake type epileptics are passive and reactive.

Muramatsu (1987), in a single case study of epilepsy, reported neurotic anxieties and concerns regarding the body in the epileptic patient. She emphasized the important role of the Rorschach test in helping such patients.

Ogawa (1980; 1981) administered the Rorschach to 18 patients diagnosed with Parkinson's disease to assess their psychological problems. The patients showed an elevated S% and a low frequency of chromatic color responses, and their Experience Balance was either introversive or coartative. He suggested that these patients had characteristics such as being reserved, self-reliant, and rigid and having an independent lifestyle.

Rorschach studies of neurological disease are declining in frequency throughout the contemporary world, and neuropsychological tests are becoming dominant in this field. This trend is also common to Japan. However, it is the author's belief that the utilization of the Rorschach test with patients suffering from neurological disturbances is warranted by the contributions the test can make to the psychological treatment of such patients.

As mentioned above, the studies cited in this paper are only a small fraction of those reported in Japan. In addition to psychological research, there are numerous Rorschach investigations in anthropology and in the literature concerning delinquency. I hope that such topics will be reviewed in this journal in the near future.

Concluding Remarks

Although the history of the Rorschach in Japan is long among the countries of the world, the history of Japanese Rorschach research is short. There are two reasons for this. One is the language barrier. Most Rorschach studies in Japan are reported in the Japanese language. As a result, foreign Rorschach scholars, who are usually unfamiliar with the Japanese language, are unaware of these studies. Although some Japanese Rorschach scholars have participated in international congresses on the Rorschach (Akitani, 1981, 1987; Ogawa, 1984, 1990; Motoaki, 1987; Nakamura & Nakamura, 1987; Nosaka & Ogawa, 1990), this modest participation has been far less than proportional to the contemporary level of Rorschach activities in Japan. Thus there is a pressing need to inform the rest of the world of the Rorschach related research activities that are taking place in Japan.

The second problem facing Japan is the lack of an official Rorschach society. Similar to the situation in the United States about 40 years ago, today in Japan there are many local workshops and associations but no responsible national organization. The lack of such an organization is an obstacle to global cooperation among Japanese workers and for workers in other countries. Happily in this respect, *Rorschachiana Japonica* has been playing an important cohesive function nationwide.

Résumé

Le Rorschach fait partie des tests psychologiques les plus employés dans le monde et tout particulièrement au Japon. Il s'agit là du résultat d'une enquête effectuée au Japon concernant l'utilisation des test psychologiques. 80 % des psychologues interrogés le considère comme un instrument indispensable à la pratique de leur métier.

Actuellement, au Japon, trois systèmes d'évaluation des réponses du Rorschach sont utilisés. À savoir:

- le système Kataguti
- celui développé à l'université d'Osaka
- celui employé à l'université de Nagoya.

Il ressort de cette même enquête que le système Kataguti est le plus communement utilisé au Japon. Il s'agit d'une modification par le Japonais du système du Klopfer qui est plus connus dans le monde.

La pluspart de la recherche effectuée sur le Rorschach est produité au Japon et est généralement répertoirée dans le *"Rorschachiana Japonica."* Rêcemment l'anorexie mentale et les troubles de la personalité limite ont éveillé l'intérêt de psychologues Japonais.

Par ailleurs, parmi les nombreuses recherches sur la psychopathologie de la schizophrénie par le Rorschach, celles concernant la réhabilitation des schizophrènes sont impressionantes; elles démontrent l'importance du Rorschach pour dresser un prognostique de l'évolution future de cette maladie.

Pendant les années 80, beaucoup de recherches ont été publiées sur l'anorexie mentale et les résultats presentent quelques concordances:

– beaucoup de réponses "K"
– peu de réponses "couleur chromatique."

Cependant, afin d'obtenir une meilleure concordance entre ces résultats, une définition plus claire de l'anorexie mentale est nécessaire.

Dans la pluspart des pays le Rorschach n'est pas considère comme utilisable pour l'évaluation des maladies neurologiques, cependant, au Japon, cette approche est très largement employée.

Il y a deux problèmes qui limitent la contribution des japonais à la recherche mondiale sur le Rorschach:

– la barrière linguistique
– l'absence d'association officielle.

La parution de la nouvelle revue *Rorschachiana* pourra aider les chercheurs japonais à surmonter des deux problèmes.

Resumen

El Rorschach es una de las pruebas psicológicas más frecuentemente utilizadas en el Japón. En una encuesta acerca del uso de las pruebas psicológicas, el Rorschach encabezó la lista; alrededor de un tercio de las personas que respondieron, la consideraron como un instrumento indispensable en su práctica cotidiana.

Tres sistemas de codificación se utilizan generalmente en el Japón: el Kataguchi, el de la Universidad de Osaka y el de la Universidad de Nagoya. La encuesta indica que el Kataguchi es el más popular. El sistema de Klopfer parece ser el más influyente entre los sistemas foráneos de codificación. Ello se debe a que el Kataguchi es, esencialmente, una modificación del sistema de Klopfer.

En el Japón, se han llevado a cabo, de manera activa, investigaciones con el Rorschach, la mayoría de las cuales son publicadas en Rorschachiana Japonica. Como una tendencia general, vienen incrementándose, en forma constante, las investigaciones clinicas con la prueba; recientemente, los trastornos borderline de la personalidad y los trastornos de la alimentación atraen la atención de los rorschachistas.

Entre los muchos estudios con el Rorschach dedicados a la esquizofrenia en la última década, resalta la investigación sobre rehabilitación de esquizofrénicos. Sus resultados han clarificado el valor de la prueba para el pronóstico de la esquizofrenia.

Durante la década de los ochenta, se reportaron varios estudios con el Rorschach en la anorexia nerviosa. Se encontraron algunos hallazgos consistentes, tales como muchas respuestas M y pocas respuestas de color cromático. Sin embargo, se requiers aún una definición conceptual más clara para avanzar en la investigación de la anorexia nerviosa a través del Rorschach.

Las investigaciones sobre perturbaciones neurológicas (i. e., epilepsia, enfermedad de Parkinson) parecen constituir una de las contribuciones propiamente japonesas, debido a que los estudios a través de Rorschach de estas afecciones han venido declinando en otras partes. Tales estudios amplían ciertamente las potencialidades de la prueba.

Varios problemas impiden aún a los estudiosos del Rorschach en Japón contribuir de lleno en el plano internacional. Uno de ellos lo constituye la barrera del idioma. Otro es la ausencia de una organización oficial para los investigadores del Rorschach. Se espera que la nueva *Rorschachiana* contribuya a resolver tales problemas.

References

Akitani, T. (1981). Rorschach responses of anorexia nervosa patients. *Rorschachiana*, XV, 65.

Akitani, T. (1987). Popular responses of Japanese and their culture. *Rorschachiana*, XVI, 104–108.

Aoki, K., & Kawai, I. (1982). Awake epilepsy and sleep epilepsy: A psychological study with Rorschach test. *Rorschachiana Japonica*, 24, 101–117. (In Japanese with English summary).

Harada, N., Kojima, T., & Shimazono, Y. (1982). A study of eye movement in schizophrenic patients during the Rorschach test: Relationship between eye movement and Rorschach score. *Rorschachiana Japonica*, 24, 13–26. (In Japanese with English summary).

Hirose, M., & Nomura, M. (1981). Changes of Rorschach pattern in chronic schizophrenia: A study of attitude to social re-adjustment. *Rorschachiana Japonica*, 23, 25–40. (In Japanese with English summary).

Ika, H., Aoki, H., & Tohyama, N. (1985). Psychopathology and psychodynamics of anorexia nervosa. *Clinical Psychiatry*, 25, 1353–1360. (In Japanese).

Kataguchi, Y. (1957). The development of the Rorschach test in Japan. *Journal of Projective Techniques*, 21, 258–260.

Motoaki, H. (1987). Development of the Rorschach application in research in Japan. *Rorschachiana*, XVI, 19–20.

Muramatsu, R. (1987). A case with epilepsy: Understanding through the Rorschach test. *Rorschachiana Japonica, 29,* 99–109. (In Japanese with English summary).

Nadaoka, T., Morioka, Y., Negishi, Y., et al. (1980). Discussion of "eating disorders" classified by types: Clinical findings and the Rorschach test. *Japanese Journal of Psychosomatic Medicine, 20,* 217–225. (In Japanese with English summary).

Nakamura, S., & Nakamura, N. (1981). The family Rorschach technique. *Rorschachiana, XVI,* 136–141.

Nosaka, M., & Ogawa, T. (1990). Rorschach scores in anorexia nervosa: What kind of changes occur when the symptoms are relieved? *Rorschachiana, XVII,* 305–307.

Ogawa, T. (1981). Rorschach test study of Parkinson's disease. *Rorschachiana Japonica, 23,* 41–55. (In Japanese with English summary).

Ogawa, T. (1984). *Some considerations on the subcategorization of vista responses.* Paper presented at the XIst International Congress of Rorschach and Projective Techniques, Barcelona, Spain.

Ogawa, T. (1990). *Les "déterminants" du Rorschach: Leur relations intimes avec les parties du discours.* Paper presented at the XIIIrd International Congress of Rorschach and Projective Techniques, Paris, France.

Ogawa, T., Yamada, Y., & Iizuka, R. (1980). Psychiatric study of the Parkinson's disease (II). *Psychiatry, 22,* 835–841. (In Japanese).

Ogawa, T., & Piotrowski, C. (1992). Clinical psychological test usage in Japan: A comparative study with a survey in U.S.A. *Tsukuba Psychological Research, 14,* 151–158. (In Japanese with English summary).

Shibata, Y., Takahashi, S., Uchida, T., et al. (1985). A study of prognostic estimation in schizophrenia with Rorschach test. *Japanese Journal of Clinical Psychiatry, 14,* 1083–1090. (In Japanese).

Shimada, K., Ito, Y., Okamura, M., et al. (1985). Psychodiagnostics of eating disorders as explored through the Rorschach test. *Journal of Japanese Clinical Psychology, 3,* 118–31. (In Japanese with English summary).

Sorai, K. (1982). Measurement of the effects of hospital treatment of schizophrenic patients by means of the Japanese modified Basic Rorschach Score. *Rorschachiana Japonica, 24,* 1–12. (In Japanese with English summary).

Takahashi, S., Shibata, Y., Kobori, S., et al. (1987). A study of prognostic estimation in schizophrenia, II: Accompanied with Rorschach test at discharge. *Japanese Journal of Clinical Psychiatry, 16,* 45–52. (In Japanese).

Tanaka, K., Takahashi, S., Tanaka, Y., & Nakamura, T. (1980). On the eye movement patterns to Rorschach inkblots. *Rorschachiana Japonica, 22,* 91–108. (In Japanese with English summary).

Tohyama, N. (1983). Psychodynamics of juvenile anorexia nervosa: A Rorschach study of twenty-five anorexic patients. *Rorschachiana Japonica, 25,* 1–18. (In Japanese with English summary).

Unai, Y., & Kato, S. (1988). The prognosis of schizophrenia: With reference to clinical evaluation with Piotrowski's Prognosis Index (short and long forms). *Rorschachiana Japonica, 30,* 97–111. (In Japanese with English summary).

The Rorschach in Finland

Carl-Erik Mattlar

The Rehabilitation Research Centre of the Social Insurance Institution, Turku, Finland

Risto Fried

University of Jyväskylä, Finland

According to the Finnish Psychological Association (Dufva, Huttunen, Härsilä, Kauppinen & Kentala, 1979), the Rorschach is, in Finland as in the U.S. (Piotrowski, 1984; Ritzler & Del Gaudio, 1976; Weiner, 1983), the personality test most used in psychodiagnostic assessment, with the Wartegg in second place. This holds true for hospitals, mental health clinics, psychiatric clinics, child guidance centers and university student health services. Psychological consultants also use it in making personnel decisions. The Rorschach usually forms part of a test battery that may also include the WAIS or WISC, drawing tests, a picture story method (CAT, TAT, ORT, or revised Finnish version of the Shneidman MAPS) and objective personality tests. The Rorschach's pre-eminence is remarkable in view of negative attitudes encountered in academic circles, and the resultant fact that a degree in psychology by no means entails competence in projective testing. In the opinion of Finnish Rorschach pioneer Aarre Tuompo (1947), it was necessary for a Finn who wanted to master the Rorschach to travel to Switzerland. Not until 1968 was an annual course devoted entirely to the Rorschach included in the curriculum of a Finnish university (Jyväskylä), and it remains the only one.

To augment their inadequate formal schooling, Finnish clinical psychologists have shown persistent initiative in organizing basic Rorschach courses and advanced seminars throughout the country. In 1971, Stephen A. Appelbaum of the Menninger Clinic was invited to hold an intensive Rorschach course. In the 1980's, Rorschach summer courses were held at Oulu University's biological research stations at the lighthouse on Hailuoto island and near the waterfalls in Oulanka National

Park. Probably the world's northernmost Rorschach seminar was held in the Lapland community of Sodankylä, annual site of the Midnight Sun Film Festival (Fried, 1978).

At the time of writing, inquiries sent to universities in neighboring countries indicate that Finland leads northern Europe in Rorschach research. In Russia, where Hermann Rorschach lived and worked in 1913–1914, his test still is not forgotten, but to obtain training, or even a set of the cards, was virtually impossible during the Soviet period. It is less obvious why Finland should have been more active in use of the Rorschach than her Scandinavian neighbors to the west. Recently Swedish psychologists have called in Finnish experts for teaching and consultation, a situation unforeseeable in Tuompo's days.

The first Rorschach plates used in Finland, as far as has been possible to determine, were in possession of the University of Helsinki in 1932. With the aid of Kai v. Fieandt (later a professor and prominent in cognitive research), K. Helasvuo (1934, 1936) wrote his Master's thesis on the Rorschach responses of male convicts in the Helsinki prison. According to Tuompo, other Rorschach studies performed during this pre-war period remained unpublished.

Depression in Front Line Soldiers

The first Finnish Rorschach study published in an international journal was Aarre Tuompo's (1947) comparison of combat servicemen with peacetime civilians. Tuompo commanded a battery on the Karelian front. After suffering heavy losses in 1941, his unit was shifted to a relatively quiet sector. Tuompo, assisted by his medical officer, made use of this lull to test 110 artillerymen (mean age 28) with the Rorschach. Returned to civilian life as a teacher in a rural area much like that from which his soldiers had been recruited, he tested a control group from among his pupils (137 men and women, mean age 18). His principal finding was that the servicemen as a group showed signs of depression as manifested in card rejections, achromatic and shading responses, detail rather than whole human responses, and morbid content (corpses, wounded men, blood, graves marked by crosses).

That men who had recently lost comrades, who were separated from their loved ones, and who lived under threat of injury or death, should show signs of depression ought not to be surprising. Yet the hero stereotype is so well established that one tends to associate clinical psychopathology only with the individual serviceman who breaks down, not with the majority who go about their duties. Tuompo's dispassionate, carefully documented account therefore comes as something of an eye opener. One wonders if this study would have made a greater impact had it been published in a journal of psychiatry rather than for an audience of German speaking Rorschach specialists.

The Intentional Fallacy

In literary criticism, the assumption that a book's meaning can be best understood in terms of what the author had intended to achieve is termed the "intentional fallacy." The term may also be useful in assessment of scientific projects.

When Kiviluoto and Heikola (1974) embarked on their study of Finnish children's Rorschach responses, they asserted that they wanted to free practicing psychologists from dependence on culture-specific U.S. norms. They tested 315 children aged 2.5 to 13 and published their findings in a book with over 300 pages of text, tables and charts. A surprising finding was that compared to the norms (Ames, Métraux, Rodell, & Walker, 1974; Ames, Métraux, & Walker, 1971) most relied on by Finnish psychologists, Finnish children consistently, at every age level, gave a higher mean total of responses. This contradicted the popular stereotype contrasting loquacious Americans with taciturn Finns. Since Ames et al.'s samples were skewed in the direction of higher than normal intelligence while Kiviluoto had scrupulously seen to it that her sample corresponded to a normal I. Q. distribution, this result seemed even more remarkable. The elevated response total affected norms for other scoring categories: Finnish children, compared with Americans, were found to have a lower W% and F+%, a higher A%.

Practicing psychologists were bewildered by these findings. The gap between test results obtained in practice and the new Finnish norms seemed far wider than had been the case with American norms. Did the lack of congruence stem from clinicians' unfamiliarity with problem-free children? Did a child tested at a guidance center differ so radically from "normal" classmates?

In an attempt to resolve this question, Dufva, Huttunen, Härsilä, Kauppinen, and Kentala (1979) tested 184 7–10 year old children and

107

112 adults, evenly divided between subjects in psychiatric treatment and nonclinical subjects. Results on productiveness differed sharply from those obtained by Kiviluoto and Heikola: for subjects aged 7–8, mean R was 17 (Kiviluoto 30 R, Ames 17 R); for subjects aged 9–10, R was 22 (Kiviluoto 39 R, Ames 17 R). According to this study, the old American norms were more useful to Finnish psychologists than Kiviluoto and Heikola's Finnish norms. Further, Dufva et al.'s findings were that differences between the "normal" and "clinical" samples, in terms of an item by item or "sign" approach to formal scoring, were small.

A likely solution to the puzzle set by the difference between the two Finnish studies was suggested by Exner's (1974) data on the relationship between administration procedures and productiveness. In the Dufva et al. study, the subject was told, if only one response was volunteered to Card I, that it was possible to give more than one response. No further exhortations were given. Kiviluoto and Heikola, in their 1974 study, emphasize the importance of giving plentiful encouragement. Just how plentiful becomes apparent only if one goes back to Kiviluoto's 1962 pilot study for a detailed account of the instructions given to testers: "The number of verbal encouragements (What else do you see? Tell me more!) was, however, for the sake of consistency, restricted to three in each picture" (p. 13). Dufva et al.'s subjects, then, were given the suggestion that they could give more responses one or zero times; Kiviluoto and Heikola's subjects, 30 times. Kiviluoto and

Heikola's intentions had been to provide Finnish clinical psychologists with useful norms, and to provide data for cross-cultural (Finland-U.S.) comparison. Instead, quite unintentionally, they succeeded in giving an impressive example of the effect of Rorschach test instructions on productivity.

Universal Normal and Cultural Specificity

In work with adults, as with children, Finnish psychologists were confronted with the questionable adequacy of the norms they used. Klopfer (Klopfer & Kelley, 1946), while acknowledging differences between cultural groups, had expressed his confidence in the universal frequency of responses common to all ages and cultures, and acceptable to every "normal" subject (p. 177–178). The majority of clinical psychologists in post-war Finland used Klopfer's norms. Norms were daily relied on in making such important decisions as whether a person was eligible for a pension, or in need of hospitalization. But the clinician rarely had experience with healthy normal people. Did a Finnish patient's deviance from Klopfer's American norms ensure psychopathology? Were Klopfer's norms valid even for the U.S., seeing that his list of P responses, for example, differed from those of other Rorschach systemizers? More than other American Rorschach authorities, Klopfer relied on clinical experience (or, to put it less politely, on subjective memory) rather than on statistics. But, to stick with the question of P responses, none of the experts who did use statistics had collected anything resembling a representative sample.

In 1975, under the auspices of the National Social Insurance Institute, Carl-Erik Mattlar (1986) and his colleagues (Mattlar, Knuts, Alanen, 1987) contacted a random sample of 650 men and women, holding out the offer of a free medical examination to participants in psychological testing. All Ss were gainfully employed. They were equally divided into five age groups (20, 30, 40, 50, and 60) and resided in five medium sized towns in various regions of Finland. The number of actual participants was 407, of whom 181 were randomly assigned to individual and 226 to group Rorschach testing. All subjects were found to be in satisfactory physical and mental health, while intelligence testing yielded a group mean in the 100–110 I. Q. range. Additionally, a sample of 108 71-year-old pensioners was tested, as were two vocation-specific groups: 56 nursing students in their early twenties, and 51 engineers and technicians in their mid-twenties. The result of this effort was that Finland, with a population of five million, now had more adequate Rorschach norms for adults than any other country. The Finnish clinician, possessed of the new handbook, can take almost any feature (R, locations, determinants, principal content categories, Experience Balance and other ratios, P) of a protocol and check its absolute or perceptual occurrence against the means and standard deviations for the appropriate sex, age group, and manner (individual or group) of administration. But the handbook is useful for foreign as well as Finnish psychologists, as succeeding tables give mean values for important elements of the structural summary for 20 other normative studies, 4 Finnish and 16 from other European countries and the United States. Additionally, tables of P responses are given for Finland as compared with the six most used American and five European studies. Finally, there is a plate by plate listing of the content of all responses given by subjects in the various Finnish normal groups, from the most popular (100%) down to originals (1% of 622 subjects).

Usefulness of these data is being further extended by rescoring in terms of Exner's Comprehensive System, as well as retesting of original subjects to supply longitudinal data after 15 years.

There is a certain irony in the finding that Klopfer was not, after all, far afield in his assertion of "universality." At least as concerns Europe and the U.S., it would seem that the principal elements of the structural summary could be described as "sturdy," little affected by nationality. Within the Finnish normal sample, differences associated with age, gender, and intelligence were small. Compared with U.S. norms, the Finnish mean R (19.7) is close to what obtains for those Americans (Exner, 21.8; Klopfer, 23.9) who least pressure testees for quantity. The Finnish random sample was a little lower on M (1.8) than Exner's normal adults (3.5). As regards P responses, the Finnish list is close to two-thirds identical with the American "consensus" list (Hertz, 1970; Exner, 1974) based on responses agreed on by three of six authors. The Finnish list comprises 14 items, and lacks 7 items from the U.S. list (e.g. butterfly or bow tie on III, human face on IX, rabbit's head and caterpillar on X). The only Finnish P not found on any U.S. list is "Christmas elves" on Card II, a uniquely Fenno-Scandinavian response that has been investigated in some detail (Fried, 1981; 1990; Mattlar, 1986).

If the Rorschach elicits so many universal response patterns and so little that is culture specific, one could be skeptical about the utility of costly, time consuming normative studies. But it is only against the background of well-established norms that one can appreciate and meaningfully investigate the diversity of group and individual responses within and between national cultures.

Take, for example, "two human beings" on Card III, one of the most popular Ps for both Finns (in Mattlar's study, 100% of technicians, 86% of student nurses, 80% of individually tested Ss in the random sample) and Americans (82% of Exner's non-psychiatric sample). The seeming cross-cultural accord is, however, only apparent. Schafer (1948, p. 156) flatly stated that the figures were male, and that to describe them as female was indicative of gender identity problems. Psychopathology or no, Americans have differed sharply (Brown, 1971; Hammer, 1966) as to the gender of the figures, while Finns of both sexes are virtually unanimous in describing them as female. The phenomenon under discussion is not restricted to information gleaned from the Rorschach. Keltikangas-Järvinen (1982) found that TAT Card 3BM, on which Americans divide fifty-fifty as to the gender of the figure portrayed, is clearly female for Finns. In administering the Shneidman MAPS, with its choice of 67 figures, psychologists found themselves stymied when Finnish testees protested that there was no adequate "Mother" figure. Dufva et al. (1979), with new female figures drawn progressively shorter and less slender than the originals, found that 75% of subjects preferred the more obese figures. To return to Card III, it was selected as best depicting "Mother" by 24.6 % of 1089 Finns individually tested with the Rorschach (Fried, 1990), while 205 Americans gave first choice (26.3%) to Card VII, which in Finland came in a poor second (15.5%). There was no cross-cultural difference in choice of a "Father" card, with both Finns (23.9%) and Americans (26.0%) giving first place to the traditional (Meer & Singer, 1950) Card IV. Findings like this one, suggestive of concepts of femininity and maternity that differ in Finnish and American cultures, are intriguing because they involve cognitive-emotional processes evocable by pictorial stimuli, but hard to explain or elicit in words. Rorschach psychology may here be capable of making a unique contribution.

Clinical and Normal: Redrawing the Boundaries

In far too many Rorschach studies, "normal" has been a wastebasket category defined only in negative terms, like not being in psychiatric treatment. A more demanding definition of normality was developed in conjunction with the University Student Health Service (Holmström, Jussila, & Vauhkonen, 1987), when it was decided to implement a thorough psychiatric and psychodiagnostic examination of a major random sample of university students. Each student was interviewed by six psychoanalytically trained psychiatrists. Not only was present functioning assessed, but subjects were followed up over a twenty year period to determine whether their life courses substantiated the original impression (Holmström, 1989). Tested with the Rorschach and compared both with Finnish (Mattlar, 1986) and American (Exner, 1986) healthy reference groups, 22 women and 17 men, initially judged to be the healthiest members of the sample, now 40 years old, were indeed found (Mattlar, Holmström, Hanses, Uotila, & Alanen, 1990) to be self-actualizers with potential for fulfilling their basic needs through use of inner resources as well as interaction with the external world. They were characterized by diversity and richness of personality, stress tolerance, ability to master overwhelming stimulation, and sound self-esteem. Compared to con-

111

trols, who were reticent and overly careful, they dared to take calculated risks in achieving maximal enjoyment of life.

With respect to the Affective Ratio (*Afr*), the healthy group achieved a higher value than the Finnish controls, but lower than the Americans. This seems consistent with the observation that the American "cocktail party" attitude of lightly controlled spontaneity is foreign to the Finnish life style, which allows of less gradations between being stone cold sober or riotously drunk.

In a companion study (Mattlar, Ruth, & Knuts, 1980–1981; Mattlar, 1986; Ruth, 1980), 407 Rorschach protocols were evaluated for creativeness as defined in terms of fluency, flexibility, and originality. Peak creativity was achieved by men in their forties and women in their twenties, possibly a function of increased educational and vocational opportunities for women in recent years. No appreciable drop-off was noted, however, even between ages 50 and 60.

Rorschach testing has, indeed, revised attitudes toward aging. As late as 1974, W. Klopfer characterized gerontological Rorschach protocols as showing signs of severe impairment: intellectual inefficiency, emotional instability, and lowered self-esteem. Though Klopfer was aware that non-institutionalized elderly subjects were not so different from younger age groups, data were generally collected from hospitals and homes for the aged. An adequate random sample of 71-year-olds (Mattlar 1986; Mattlar, Knuts, & Virtanen,1985; Mattlar, Carlsson, Forsander, Karppi, & Helenius, 1991) living at home revealed that they differed markedly little from younger groups. For the majority, energy resources, level of percept formation, critical thinking, sense of reality, social awareness, and capacity for emotional response were intact. An ongoing (Mattlar, Carlsson, Forsander, Norrlund, Karppi, Helenius, & Make, in preparation) study of non-patient octogenarians confirms results arrived at in France (Poitrenaud & Moreaux, 1975): although difficulties in perception-mediational functioning and signs of depression have increased, about half still have a personality structure comparable with that of non-patient adults.

Related to the question of personality deterioration with advancing age is that of cerebral dysfunction. Piotrowski (1937) accomplished the first Rorschach scale for evaluating cerebral dysfunction in terms of impaired percept formation. After decades of research, the Piotrowski scale has continued to lead the field (Goldfried, Stricker, & Weiner, 1971; Lezak, 1976/83). It produces few false positives and a score of 5 or more usually discloses cerebral impairment. The question has re-

112

mained whether the test's sensitivity results in high scores being prevalent even in the general population. Using data from the Finnish random sample (Mattlar, 1986), it was found (Mattlar, Knuts & Alanen, 1986) that scores of more than 5 were rare up to age 40, but characterized every fourth 50-year-old and every third 60-year-old. Association with intelligence (excepting the WAIS Digit Symbol subtest) was slight, but factor analysis revealed three factors: (a) impaired speed of perception formation; (b) hesitancy, rigidity; and (c) difficulty in coping with emotion. These were individuals, however, who complained of no disease and functioned relatively well in the community. The phenomenon may hence be associated with normal biological aging or due to small cardiovascular incidents from which one thinks one has recovered. As Piotrowski himself (1937) was careful to point out, a high score need not signify major impairment, but must be interpreted in the context of the entire Rorschach record.

Clinical Studies

Confronted by a major dilemma, the optimist asserts that the situation is serious, but not hopeless, whereas the cynic smiles that it is hopeless, but not serious. Depending on one's point of view, it may seem a tragic, or merely an absurd, waste of resources that thousands of Rorschach records are locked away in the files of hospitals and clinics while the researcher interested in a specific diagnostic group must laboriously search out and test enough individuals to accumulate a sample big enough – just and just – to satisfy the demands of statistical credibility. In Finland and Sweden, institution of Rorschach Workshops and changeover to the Comprehensive System (Exner 1986, 1990, 1991) aims at becoming part of a world-wide data bank that will enable the clinician of the future, each time a Rorschach has been administered, to deposit its contents in the bank, receiving in return a ready written diagnostic report based on all reference groups pertinent to the case just deposited. But while waiting for the millennium (only 8 more years to 2000 A. D.), Rorschach psychologists must make do with research results based on relatively small groups.

Using psychiatric interviews and the consensus Rorschach, Alanen and Kinnunen (1974) studied the relationships of 30 couples in which one spouse had become schizophrenic subsequent to marriage. They distinguished three basic types: (a) a dependent, passive schizophrenic spouse with a pathogenic, dominant partner; (b) schizophrenic and non-schizophrenic partners in a relationship of mutual symbiotic clinging; and (c) a dominating schizophrenic spouse with a more realistic, but dependent partner. Findings indicated that the first type of relationship benefited more from individual than from couples therapy. The second and third types, with a better overall prognosis, gained from couples therapy.

Keltikangas-Järvinen (1984) and her associates (e. g. Keltikangas-Järvinen, Ruokolainen, & Lehtonen, 1982; Keltikangas-Järvinen, Mueller, & Lehtonen, 1989) have used content scales to demonstrate that chronic prostatitis sufferers showed personality defects possibly associated with disturbed interpersonal relationships in infancy. Following up patients' responses to surgery, they found (Keltikangas-Järvinen, Loven, & Möller, 1984) that long-term adaptation was better for ileostomy than for colostomy.

Results of in-patient treatment for borderline patients have been investigated (Antikainen, 1990) using the Lerner Defense Scale. While there was no difference in frequency of resort to primitive defenses (devaluation, idealization, denial) at beginning and end of treatment, there was a tendency for these defenses to be used in less extreme forms. This suggests that, while brief treatment did not change essential personality pathology, it resulted in better capacity for adjustment and coping.

Wahlström (1987) used the Concensus Rorschach to test the hypothesis that a pattern of interaction specific to psychosomatic families characterized families with an asthmatic child. He found not one, but several divergent patterns.

Other studies of dysfunctional groups have focused on obesity (Ihanus, Keltikangas-Järvinen, & Mustajoki, 1986; Mattlar, Salminen, & Alanen, 1989; Mattlar, Carlsson, Salminen, Vesala, Mäki, & Alanen, 1990); intermittent claudication (Keltikangas-Jarvinen, Lepantalo, & Lindfors, 1987;

Keltikangas-Jarvinen, Lidfors, & Lepantalo, 1987); interstitial cystitis (Keltikangas-Jarvinen, Auvinen, & Lehtonen, 1988); personality differences between good and poor sleepers (Mattlar & Kronholm, 1990; Mattlar, Carlsson, Kronholm, Rytöhonka, Santasalo, Hyyppä, Mäki, & Alanen, 1991); families with an alcohol problem (Fried, Halme, Jalonen, Keskitalo, & Suokas, 1983); and various cerebral lesions (Vilkki, 1978, 1981, 1987).

Further, there have been case studies exploring the sensation of flying in Rorschach responses, dreams and behavior as related to fantasized omnipotence, and fears of falling or loss of ego cohesion in skyjackers and faith healers (Fried, 1980, 1982, 1984; Fried, Rantasila, Reinikainen, Malkavaara-Kallinen, & Huttunen, 1988; Fried & Reinikainen, 1983).

The Cookbook and the Jungle

When interpreting content in a Rorschach record, many clinicians commit either of two sins: reliance on ready-made conclusions furnished by an authority (the "cookbook" approach), or giving their own intuitions free play ("wild analysis"). Though these may seem like opposite extremes, they have in common uncritical acceptance of conclusions that have not been checked out against the Highest Authority: the testee.

Anne Lyytinen and Riitta Nortala (1987) investigated the adequacy of well thumbed cookbooks, such as Phillips and Smith (1953), for gaining an understanding of animal responses of Finnish first year university students. Most of the cookbook writers fared quite well, in the sense that a majority of subjects usually expressed feelings that coincided with the standard interpretation. There was, however, a great deal of variation even within Lyytinen and Nortala's relatively small ($n = 40$) and homogeneous sample. First, it was found that whereas affective response to some animals was near-unanimous (rats were loathsome), others provoked markedly different responses in different subjects (lions as frightening or as noble, highly admired animals). A bear reminded a student from an urban area of the teddy bear to which she clung for security when going to sleep as a child; a student from Lapland saw bears as cruel predators that endanger reindeer herders' livelihood. In addition to inter-subject variability, there was intra-subject variability, as measured by a scale for ambivalence and intensity of feeling. The reasons underlying inconsistent reaction to a particular animal became clearer through free verbalizations. Subjects frequently began with adult, rational attitudes based on knowledge (wolves as an endangered species in need of protection), then revealed contradictory attitudes based on childhood emotion. One man, for example, described bats as useful destroyers of harmful insects, then continued "This bat seems to be looking (white spaces on Card I as eyes) right at me – but why should I be afraid? I'm not an insect."

A third factor in variability resided in interaction between subjective responses and the stimulus properties of the cards. Many Rorschach psychologists consider bat and butterfly responses to I and V as equivalent, and diagnostically uninformative, responses. Lyytinen and Nortala found that most subjects connected the bat on V, small and with good form-concept fit, with more positive feelings than the big, dark, dysphoric and "mystical" bat on I. A butterfly on III was apperceived as cheerful and carefree, but a butterfly on I or V, because of the dissonance between the card's form and blackness and what a butterfly should be, aroused anxious and depressive feeling even more than a bat response to the same card. Phillips and Smith's interpretation of spiders as "dominating and possessive mother figures" (p. 122) received support when a spider had been perceived in an unusual area, but not for the *P* spider on X, where the response can be "read" from the card without personal involvement. Generally, then, the meaning of *A* responses did not reside in the concept of an animal per se, but in its interrelationship with each card's unique properties. Even this rule, however, was not always useful, as some subjects were so preoccupied with a problem (e. g. achieving independence from home) that they repeatedly expressed it, using any animal on any card as a mere vehicle for their overriding concern. Lyytinen and Nortala's investigation, then, reminds us of what we should have known all along: the content of a response deserves inquiry as careful as that accorded locations and determinants. The psychologist should never assume that he or she knows what the testee has in mind without needing to ask.

When Not To Use the Rorschach

A patient repeatedly hospitalized during manic episodes told the psychologist who wanted to administer the Rorschach that she had taken it so often, she could do it with her eyes closed. Indeed she produced a long record, with responses appropriate to each card, strictly from memory, without once opening her eyes.

Even without experiences as dramatic as this, psychologists sometimes feel the need for an alternative technique. In response to a suggestion from Z. Mahmood, editor of the *British Journal of Projective Psychology*, an international team (Mattlar, Sandahl, Lindberg, Lehtinen, Carlsson, Vesala, & Mahmood, 1990; Ruth, Aberg, Mattlar, Sandahl, Oist, Carlsson, & Vesala, 1990; Sandahl, Mattlar, Carlsson, Vesala, & Rosenquist, 1990; Uhinki, Mattlar, Sandahl, Vesala, & Carlsson, 1990) set about "Exnerizing" the three-inkblot Zulliger so as to standardize its administration and scoring, and provide norms that would make it a viable alternative to the Rorschach. While the Zulliger's stimulus properties and brevity are incompatible with its use as a test strictly parallel with and equivalent to the Rorschach, it could be used as an independent test that can be interpreted utilizing Rorschach principles, and yielding similar results in such areas as vocational choices, clinical diagnosis, and cross-cultural comparison.

Conclusion

We have followed the Rorschach in Finland from its adoption in the 1930's through its baptism of fire on the Karelian front and on through a period of symbiotic dependence – normal in infancy – on the mother (the U. S. A.), the father having died too early to give much guidance. In early attempts at individuation, seeking a national identity, the child perhaps rebelled too strongly, and overemphasized its difference from the parents. Now a period of rapprochement (Mahler, Pine, & Bergman, 1975) has set in. Secure in its sense of independence, confident of having something of value to give, the Finnish Rorschach is also willing to acknowledge commonalities and eager to communicate and coöcooperate not only with parents, but with the peer group.

Résumé

Le Rorschach est le test de personnalité le plus utilisé en Finlande. Bien qu'il soit appréhendé avec scepticisme dans les milieux académiques, le Rorschach est enseigné dans des cours qu'organisent les psychologues praticiens de leur propre initiative. Dans le domaine des publications zur le Rorschach, la Finlande fait figure de chef de file, en comparaison avec la Scandinavie et la Russie, ses voisins nord-européens. La première étude finlandaise, rapportée dans Rorschachiana (1947), analysait les réponses de combattants qui se trouvaient sur le front. Le rejet des planches, la couleur achromatique et les contenus morbides signalaient l'existence d'une dépression très répandue, découverte qui contredisait l'image publique des combattants finlandais, mais qui suggérait bien la sensibilité du Rorschach à des traits peu évidents dans le comportement observé.

Plusieurs études se sont préoccupées de la mise au point de normes finlandaises, en les distinguant de celles disponibles pour d'autres cultures. Une recherche initiale selon laquelle les enfants finlandais étaient beaucoup plus productifs que les Américains créa un effet de surprise, jusqu'à ce qu'une révision de la méthode révèle que les chercheurs avaient demandé aux sujets examinés de donner davantage de réponses (jusqu'à 30 exhortations par protocole). Lorsque la passation du test devenait conforme à la pratique clinique, le nombre de réponses chutait et correspondait alors au taux international. Des études plus tardives s'appesantirent sur des variables démographiques, fournissant des normes plus détaillées et plus fidèles que celles disponibles pour d'autres nationalités. La comparaison entre les normes finlandaises et américaines ne révéla que des différences mineures dans le résumé structural ainsi qu'une superposition de deux-tiers pour les banalités. Toutefois, cette ressemblance inter-culturelle joue davantage sur le plan de la dénotation que celui de la connotation. Ainsi, les Finlandais, comme les Américains, décrivent la planche III comme deux êtres humains en activité, mais les premiers perçoivent ces personnages comme plus féminins et maternels.

En Finlande, la centration des recherches Rorschach s'est progressivement détachée d'une préoccupation exagérée avec la psychopathologie. Des suppositions pessimistes concernant la détérioration du fonctionement mental avec le vieillissement ont dû être révisées, lorsque des échantillons aléatoires de septagénaires et d'octogénaires ont permis d'inclure des sujets vivant à la maison et non pas seulement des sujets institutionalisés. Dans une étude longitudinale, psychiatres et Rorschachiens ont conjointement examiné la présence d'une bonne santé mentale, telle qu'elle peut s'exprimer à travers une personnalité riche et diverse, une tolérance au stress et une estime de soi solide.

La pratique du Rorschach avec consensus s'est utilisée pour planifier des thérapies de couples et de familles, au sein desquel(le)s l'on comptait un sujet diagnostiqué comme schizophrénique, alcoolique ou asthmatique. Par ailleurs, des études de cas individuels ont fourni un aperçu des motivations régnant parmi les individus qui détournent des avions et ceux qui se proclament guérisseurs ou encore sorciers.

Une autre étude, consacrée aux réponses animales, recommande la pratique d'une enquête patiente et non-structurée qui ne s'appuye ni sur des "recettes de cuisine" ni sur l'intuition subjective de l'examinateur.

En effet, le même animal peut détenir des significations très différentes d'un sujet à l'autre, voire pour un même sujet, lorsque celui-ci peut être amené à régresser depuis une connaissance factuelle jusqu'à des fantasmes remontant à l'enfance.

Enfin, l'adoption à l'échelle nationale du Système Synthétique est en train de faciliter une coopération internationale.

Resumen

El Rorschach es la prueba de personalidad más utilizada en Finlandia. Aunque considerada con escepticismo en los circulos académicos, viene siendo enseñada en cursos organizados, bajo su propia iniciativa, por psicólogos practicantes. En cuanto a la investigación publicada con el Rorschach, Finlandia lideriza a sus vecinos de Europa del Norte, los países escandinavos y Rusia. El primer estudio finlandés reportado en Rorschachiana (1947) analizó las respuestas de soldados combatientes, a los cuales se le administró la prueba en el frente de batalla. Los rechazos, el color acromático y el contenido mórbido indicaban considerable depresión – un hallazgo contrastante con la imagen pública de los combatientes finlandeses, pero que sugiere la sensibilidad del Rorschach a rasgos que no se evidencian rápidamente en la conducta observable –.

La preocupación por obtener datos normativos finlandeses, en comparación con los datos disponibles de otras culturas, se observa en varios estudios. Los hallazgos tempranos acerca de que los niños finlandeses eran mucho más productivos que los americanos fueron recibidos con sorprese, hasta que una revisión del método reveló que los investigadores habian solicitado a los examinados que dieran respuestas adicionales, a razón de 30 exhortaciones por protocolo. Cuando se administró el test en conformidad con la práctica clinica, el número de respuestas disminuyó a los niveles conocidos internacionalmente. Estudios subsiguientes prestaron especial atención a las variables demográficas, aportando normas más confiables y detalladas que las disponibles actualmente para otras nacionalidades. La comparación de las normas finlandesas con las normas americanas revela solamente diferencias menores en el sumario estructural, y un solapamiento en dos tercios de las respuestas populares. La similaridad transcultural, sin embargo, se mantiene mejor en el nivel denotativo que en el nivel connotativo. Los finlandeses, como los americanos, describen, en la Lámina III, dos seres humanos activos, pero los finlandeses perciben las figuras como más femeninas y maternales.

En Finlandia, el excesivo interés por la psicopatología como foco del Rorschach se ha venido desplazando. Los presupuestos pesimistas acerca del deterioro del funcionamiento mental con el avance de la edad han sido revisados, cuando las muestras aleatorias de sujetos septuagenarios y octogenarios incluyeron sujetos que vivían en sus hogares, y no solamente internados en instituciones. La salud mental positiva, tal como se expresa a través de la diversidad y riqueza de la personalidad, la tolerancia al estrés y la solidez en la autoestima, ha sido estudiada conjuntamente por psiquiatras y psicólogos rorschachistas en un estudio longitudinal.

El Rorschach consensual ha sido utilizado en la planificación del tratamiento con pareras o familias que incluyen un miembro diagnosticado como esquizofrénico, alcohólico o asmático. Estudios de casos individuales han aportado luces acerca de las motivaciones de secuestradores de aviones, personas que ofrecen curar a través de la fé y brujos.

Un estudio de respuestas animales enfatiza la conveniencia de una encuesta abierta, no apresurada, en oposición al apoyo en generalizaciones del tipo "recetario", o intuiciones subjetivas del examinador. El mismo animal puede tener significados marcadamente diferentes para distintos sujetos – o aún para uno solo y el mismo sujeto, cuando se le permite regresar del conocimiento de hechos a fantasias que remiten a la infancia –.

En Finlandia, la conversión al Sistema Comprensivo, a todo lo largo del pais, está facilitando la cooperación internacional.

References

Alanen, Y.O., & Kinnunen, P. (1974). Marriage and the development of schizophrenia. *Psychiatrica Fennica, 5,* 121–143.

Ames, L. B., Métraux, R. W., Rodell, J. L., & Walker, R. N. (1974). *Child Rorschach responses* (rev. ed.). New York: Brunner/Mazel.

Ames, L.B., Métraux, R.W., & Walker, R.N. (1971). *Adolescent Rorschach responses* (rev. ed.). New York: Brunner/Maazel.

Antikainen, R. (1990). Rajatilapotilaiden yhteisöhoidon Rorschach-seuranta (A Rorschach follow-up study of the outcome of hospital treatment of borderline patients). *Psykologia, 25* (5), 354–362, 422.

Beck, S.J., Rabin, A.I., Thiesen, W.G., Molish, H., & Thetford, W.N. (1950). The normal personality as projected in the Rorschach test. *Journal of Psychology 30*, 241-298.

Brown, F. (1971). Changes in sexual identification and role over a decade and their implications. *Journal of Psychology*, 77, 229-251.

Dufva, J., Huttunen, A., Härsilä, M., Kauppinen, U., & Kentala, S. (1979). *Rorschach musteläiskätesti Suomessa* (The Rorschach inkblot test in Finland). Unpublished master's thesis, University of Jyväskylä, Finland.

Exner, J.E., Jr. (1974) *The Rorschach: A comprehensive system.* New York: Wiley.

Exner, J.E., Jr. (1986). *The Rorschach: A comprehensive system. Volume 1, Basic Foundations* (2nd ed.). New York: Wiley.

Exner, J.E., Jr. (1990). *A Rorschach Workbook for the Comprehensive* System (3rd ed.). Asheville, N. C.: Rorschach Workshops.

Exner, J.E. (1991). *The Rorschach: A Comprehensive System. Volume 2: Interpretation* (2nd ed.). New York: Wiley.

Fried, R. The emotional significance of nature for children living in Lapland (Abstract). In *Scientific and Technical Progress and Circumpolar Health* (Vol. 1, p. 250). Novosibirsk: USSR Academy of Medical Sciences.

Fried, R. (1980). Rorschach and Icarus. In J.S. Kwawer, H.D. Lerner, P.M. Lerner & A. Sugarman (Eds), *Borderline phenomena and the Rorschach test* (pp. 107-132). New York: International Universities.

Fried, R. (1981). Christmas elves on the Rorschach: A popular Finnish response and its cultural significance. *Rorschachiana*, *14*, 114.

Fried, R. (1982). The psychology of the terrorist. In B.M. Jenkins (Ed.), *Terrorism and beyond* (pp. 119-124). Santa Monica, CA: Rand.

Fried, R. (1984). Icarian personality in psychology and the arts. In H. Bonarius, G. Van Heck & N. Smid (Eds.), *Personality psychology in Europe* (pp. 349-367). Lisse, The Netherlands: Swets & Zeitlinger.

Fried, R. (1990). *Stimulus character in the Rorschach inkblots* (Report No. 274). Jyväskylä, Finland: University of Jyväskylä, Department of Psychology.

Fried, R., Halme, S., Jalonen, L., Keskitalo, P., & Suokas, A. (1983). The diagnostic team and the alcoholic family. In W.-R. Minsel & Herff (Eds.), *Research on psychotherapeutic approaches* (pp. 284-290). Frankfurt a. M., Bern, New York: Peter Lang.

Fried, R., Rantasila, E., Reinikainen, M., Malkavaara-Kallinen, E., & Huttunen, M-H. (1988). The paradox of pregenitality: Longing for contact, fear of intimacy. In H.D. Lerner & P.M. Lerner (Eds.), *Primitive mental states and the Rorschach* (pp. 3-51). Madison, CT: International Universities.

Fried, R., & Reinikainen, M. (1983). *Witchcraft in a modern urban community: Rorschach-MMPI analysis of a "good witch."* Paper presented at the 8th International Conference on Personality Assessment, Copenhagen, August.

Goldfried, M.R., Stricker, G., & Weiner, I.B. (1971). *Rorschach handbook of clinical and research applications.* Englewood Cliffs, NJ: Prentice Hall.

Hammer, M. (1966). A comparison of responses by clinic and norma adults to Rorschach card III figure area. *Journal of Projective Techniques and Personality Assessment, 30*, 161-162.

Helasvuo, K. (1934). *Tutkimuksia syklotyymisillä ja skit sotyymisillä väkivaltarikoksen tekijöillä.* HY. Sosiologian laitos.

Helasvuo, K. (1936). *Tutkimuksia Kretschmerin typologiasta II. 2. Tutkimuksia väkivaltarikollisilla.* Ajatus VIII, 118-170.

Hertz, M.R. (1970). *Frequency tables for scoring Rorschach responses* (rev. ed.). Cleveland & London: Press of Case Western Reserve University.

Holmström, R. (1989). Healthy students as adult citizens. Comparison of healthy and ill minorities. *Acta Psychiatrica Scandinavica, 80*, Suppl. 351.

Holmström, R., Jussila, L., & Vauhkonen, K. (1987). Assessment of mental health and illness, considered in the light of a 13-year longitudinal study. *Acta Psychiatrica Scandinavica, 75*, Suppl. 333.

Ihanus, J., Keltikangas-Järvinen, L., & Mustajoki, P. (1986). Preliminary remarks on the psychodynamics underlying morbid obesity. *The British Journal of Projective Psychology and Personality Study 31*, 16-24.

Keltikangas-Järvinen, L. (1982). *TAT:n ohjekirja: suomalaisia tuloksia* (TAT guidebook: Finnish results). Helsinki. Psykologien Kustannus.

Keltikangas-Järvinen, L. (1984). Sexual disorders in chronic prostatitis reflected in projective tests. *The British Journal of Projective Psychology and Personality Study, 29* (1), 9-11.

Keltikangas-Järvinen, L. (1986). Psychological meaning of illness and coping with disease. *Psychotherapy and Psychosomatics, 45*, 84-90.

Keltikangas-Järvinen, L., Auvinen, L., & Lehtonen, T. (1988). Psychological factors related to interstitial cystitis. *European Urology 15*, 69-72.

Keltikangas-Järvinen, L., Lepäntalo, M., & Lindfors, O. (1987a). Personality factors as predictors of compliance with ant the outcome of supervised self-care program for patients with intermittent claudication. *Scand. J. Rehab. Med., 19*, 1-6.

Keltikangas-Järvinen, L., Lindfors, O., & Lepäntalo, M. (1987b). Personality factors in intermittent claudication related to the outcome of self-care program. *Scand J Rehab Med 19*, 7-11.

Keltikangas-Järvinen, L., Loven, E., & Möller, C. (1984). Psychic factors determining the long-term adaptation of colostomy and ileostomy patients. *Psychotherapy and Psychosomatics, 41*, 153-159.

Keltikangas-Järvinen, L., Mueller, K., & Lehtonen, T. (1989). Illness behavior and personality changes in patients with chronic prostatitis during a two-year follow-up period. *European Urology, 16*, 181-184.

Keltikangas-Järvinen, L., Ruokolainen, J., & Lehtonen, T. (1982). Personality pathology underlying chronic prostatitis. *Psychotherapy and Psychosomatics, 37*, 87-95.

Kiviluoto, H. (1962). *Trends of development in Rorschach responses* (Report No. B-83). Turku, Finland: Turku University

Kiviluoto, H., & Heikola, R. (1974). *Rorschachin testin kehitysdiagnostinen käsikirja* (A developmental diagnostic handbook for the Rorschach test). Turku, Finland: Turku University, Department of Psychology.

Kiviluoto, H., & Heikola, R. (1981). *Rorschachin testin kehitysdiagnostinen käsikirja* (A developmental diagnostic handbook for the Rorschach test). Turku: Department of Psychology, University of Turku.

Klopfer, B., & Kelley, D.M. (1946). *The Rorschach technique.* Yonkers, NY: World Book.

Klopfer, W.G. (1974). The Rorschach and old age. *Journal of Personality Assessment, 38,* 420–422.

Kohut, H. (1971). *The analysis of self.* New York: International Universities Press.

Lezak, M.D. (1976/1983). *Neuropsychological assessment* (2nd ed.). New York: Oxford University Press.

Lyytinen, A. & Nortala, R. (1987). *Rorschachin eläinvastausten persoonallisista merkityksistä* (On the personal meaning of Rorschach animal responses). Unpublished master's thesis, University of Jyväskylä, Finland.

Mahler, M.S., Pine, F., & Bergman, A. (1975). *The psychological birth of the human infant.* New York: Basic Books.

Mattlar, C.-E. (1986) *Finnish Rorschach responses in cross-cultural context: A normative study.* Jyväskylä: Jyväskylä Studies in Education, Psychology and Social Research, 58, diss.

Mattlar, C.-E., Carlsson, A., Salminen, J.K., Vesala, P., Mäki, J., & Alanen, E. (1990a). *Personality structure for morbidly obese persons, evaluated using the Rorschach. A 5 year follow-up.* XIIIth International Congress of Rorschach and Projective Techniques, July 22–27, Paris. Abstract published.

Mattlar, C.-E., Carlsson, A., Kronholm, E., Rytöhonka, R., Santasalo, H., Hyyppä, M.T., Mäki, J., & Alanen, E. (1991a). Sleep disturbances in a community sample investigated by means of the Rorschach. *British Journal of Projective Psychology, 36* (2), 15–34.

Mattlar, C.-E., Carlsson, A., Forsander, C., Karppi, S.-L., & Helenius, H. (1991b). *Rorschach and old age; Personality characteristics for a group physically fit 80-year-old men.* 1st Scientific Meeting of the ERA, Paris, September 7h. To be printed.

Mattlar, C.-E., Holmström, R., Hanses, O., Uotila. H., & Alanen, E. (1990b). *Rorschach results for a group mentally healthy persons.* XIIIth International Congress of Rorschach and Projective Techniques, July 22–27, Paris. Abstract published.

Mattlar, C.-E., Knuts, L.-R., & Virtanen, E. (1985). Personality structure on the Rorschach for a group of healthy 71-year-old females and males. *The British Journal of Projective Psychology and Personality Study, 30* (1), 3–8.

Mattlar, C.-E., Knuts, L.-R., & Alanen, E. (1986). The Piotrowski sign system: Its association with age and intelligence, and the structure of the Piotrowski signs. *British Journal of Projective Psychology, 31* (1), 3–15.

Mattlar, C.-E., Knuts, L-R. & Alanen, E. (1987). The essential features of the Rorschach in cross-cultural context: A normative study. *Rorschachiana XVI,* 95–103.

Mattlar, C.-E., & Kronholm, E. (1990). Quality of sleep and projective methods. *Revue de Psychologie Appliquée, 40* (2), 165–178.

Mattlar, C.-E., Ruth, J.-E., & Knuts, L.-R. (1980–81). Creativity measured by the Rorschach test in relation to age in a random sample of Finns. *The Geron XXIII Yearbook, 23,* 15–26.

Mattlar, C.-E., Salminen, J.K., & Alanen, E. (1989). Rorschach findings for the extremely obese: Results from a two-year reducing programme. *British Journal of Projective Psychology, 34* (1): 2–27.

Mattlar, C.-E., Sandahl, C., Lindberg, S., Lehtinen, V., Carlsson, A., Vesala, P., & Mahmood, Z. (1990c). Methodological issues associated with the Comprehensive System when analysing the Zulliger, and the structural resemblance between the Zulliger and the Rorschach. *British Journal of Projective Psychology, 35* (2), 17–37.

Meer, B., & Singer L.J. (1950). A note on the "father" and "mother" cards in the Rorschach inkblots. *Journal of Consulting Psychology, 14,* 482–484.

Nieminen, S. (1984). *Teachers' perception of mental health, its relationship to their mental health and to changes thereof.* Helsinki: Department of Teacher Education, University of Helsinki, Research Report 27, diss.

Phillips, L., & Smith, J.G. (1953). *Rorschach interpretation: Advanced technique.* New York: Grune & Stratton.

Piotrowski, C. (1984). The status of projective techniques: or "Wishing won't make it go away". *Journal of Clinical Psychology, 40* (6), 1495–1501.

Piotrowski, Z. (1937). The Rorschach inkblot method in organic disturbances of the central nervous system. *Journal of Nervous and Mental Disease, 86* (5), 525–537.

Poitrenaud, J., & Moreaux, C. (1975). Responses données au test de Rorschach par une groupe de sujets agées, cliniquement normaux. *Revue de Psychologie Appliquée, 25* (4), 267–284.

Ritzler, B.A. & Del Gaudio, A.C. (1976). A survey of Rorschach teaching in APA-approved clinical graduate programs. *Journal of Personality Assessment, 40* (5), 451–453.

Ritzler, B., & Nalesnik, D. (1990). The effect of the inquiry on the Exner Comprehensive System. *Journal of Personality Assessment, 55* (3/4), 647–656.

Rorschach, H. (1921). *Psychodiagnostik.* Bern: Hans Huber.

Ruth, J.-E. (1980). *Creativity as a cognitive construct: The effects of age, sex and testing practice.* Diss. at the Andrus Gerontology Center, University of Southern California.

Ruth, J.-E., Åberg, P., Mattlar, C-E., Sandahl, Ch., Öist, A.-S., Carlsson, A., & Vesala, P. (1990). Old age and loneliness illustrated by the Zulliger. *British Journal of Projective Psychology, 35* (2), 61–73.

Sandahl, Ch., Mattlar, C.-E., Carlsson, A., Vesala, P., & Rosenquist, A. (1990). The personality structure for the normal adult, as revealed by the Zulliger. *British Journal of Projective Psychology, 35* (2), 54–60.

Schafer, R. (1948). *The clinical application of psychological tests.* New York: International Universities.

Schneider, E. (1929). Die Bedeutung des Rorschach'schen Formdeutversuches zur Ermittlung intellektuell gehemmter Schüler. *Zeitschrift für angewandte Psychologie, 32*, 102–163.

Schneider, E. (1936). *Psychodiagnostisches Praktikum für Psychologen und Pädagogen.* Leipzig: Johann Ambrosius Barth.

Seitamo, L. (1988). Trends in school achievement in Skolt Lappish and northern Finnish children as a function of cultural and psychological factors. *Circumpolar Health, 87, Arctic Medical Research*, 97–101.

Seitamo, L. (1980). Psychic development in Skolt Lapp children. *Nordisk psykologi, 32* (2), 166–168.

Tuompo, A. (1947). Erfahrungen mit dem Rorschachversuch an der finnischen Front (Experiences with the Rorschach on the Finnish front). *Rorschachiana, 2*, 114–122.

Uhinki, A., Mattlar, C.-E., Sandahl, Ch., Vesala, P., & Carlsson, A. (1990). Personality traits characteristic for adolescents highlighted by the Zulliger. *British Journal of Projective Psychology, 35* (2), 49–53.

Vilkki, J. (1978). Effect of thalamic lesions on complex perception and memory. *Neuropsychologia, 16*, 427–437.

Vilkki, J. (1981). Changes in complex perception and memory after three different psychosurgical operations. *Neuropsychologia, 19* (4), 553–563.

Vilkki, J. (1987). Ideation and memory in the inkblot technique after focal cerebral lesions. *Journal of Clinical and Experimental Neuropsychology, 9* (6), 699–710.

Wahlström, J. (1987). Consensus Rorschach interaction patterns of families with an asthmatic child. *Journal of Family Therapy, 9*, 265–280.

Weiner, I.B. (1983). The future of psychodiagnosis revisited. *Journal of Personality Assessment, 47* (5), 451–459.

The Comprehensive System in the Netherlands

Jan Derksen

Catholic University of Nijmegen, The Netherlands

Leo Cohen

Free University Hospital, Amsterdam, The Netherlands

Corine de Ruiter

University of Amsterdam, The Netherlands

From the 1940's through the beginning of the 1960's, a psychological investigation in the Netherlands consisted in principal of three parts: an investigation of intelligence (for instance by means of the WAIS); an assessment of personality (very often the MMPI); and a projective technique (very often the Rorschach). These test results together with the case history were the most important resources for writing a psychological report. At this time the psychological report was incomplete if it did not contain the results of the Rorschach test. The leading theoretical orientations of the Dutch psychologists were phenomenological, humanistic, and to a smaller extent psychoanalytic. In this tradition the Rorschach was used as an instrument to assess the unique human psychological characteristics.

During the 1940s and the 1950s interest in the Rorschach was common and widespread (De Zeeuw, 1986). Publications in the Netherlands on the Rorschach did not appear until 25 years after the publication of Hermann Rorschach's book "Psychodiagnostik" (1921). The first Dutch book that reviewed Rorschach data was published by De Zeeuw in 1952. Teaching the Rorschach at the university was not common, but in the 1950s specialists were appointed to familiarize the students with the scoring and interpretation of the Rorschach. Despite this interest, it is striking that until now there has never been published a manual in the

Netherlands, and, apart from some smaller samples, no norms have been established.

Starting in the beginning of the 1960s the academic climate changed. From the United States the empirical scientific paradigm spread to the Netherlands and in clinical psychology this coincided with the arrival of behaviorism and learning theory. Phenomenological and psychoanalytic theory were sent to the rear of the academic stage. Empirical research became a major issue, and learning and cognitive theories could be operationalized easier than the vague phenomenological and psychodynamic notions.

By the late 1960's the Rorschach test was no longer taken seriously by leading academicians in the Netherlands. The criticism of American empirically oriented psychologists (Cronbach, 1949) and a dissertation by Van Riemsdijk (1964) in the Netherlands had had a chilling effect on Dutch psychologists responsible for the teaching of psychodiagnosis. Apart from the academic climate, the Rorschach presented several problems for the clinical psychologists. The systems of Beck and Klopfer were popular, but these approaches presented several difficulties. Systematic and officially recognized training in administration, scoring and interpretation was lacking, the systems showed contradictions, and reliability and validity were not meeting accepted standards. The practitioner in the Netherlands employed the Rorschach in a way that was determined by his or her own clinical experience. In large parts of the clinical field the Rorschach was used in "a clinical way," which meant that no scoring or interpretation was completed. The psychologist examined the responses the patients gave to the blots and generated hypotheses about the patients' problems and personality, against the background of the data from the case history. Systematic scoring and interpretation was considered overly time consuming. Experienced clinicians emphasized the projective aspects of the technique.

For at least 20 years in the academic world the Rorschach was presented as a curious relic from psychology's past. Students were taught to disregard it, and the plates graced the walls of more than one notable scholar as intriguing decorations or as objects of humor. Though largely written off in academic circles, the Rorschach continued to be used in clinical settings (Evers & Zaal, 1979). In 1988, Bovenhoff, van Kemenade, de Ruiter & Cohen reported the results of a survey investigating the use of the Rorschach in clinical settings in the Netherlands. Of the 195 respondents 60 % reported that the Rorschach had been administered in their department or service institution. More than half of the respondents reported that the test was still in use in the year that was the focus of the survey. The Rorschach figured in more than half of the cases of psychological assessment. If an interpretation system was used, is was mainly Klopfer's and Beck's.

During the last 30 years an impressive number of psychological tests and questionnaires has been added to the three aspects of the psychological investigation mentioned above. In addition, numerous psychological techniques have been introduced in neuropsychology. For research purposes a great many semi-structured interviews and questionnaires have been developed, focussing on many features and details of human functioning and experience. The development of questionnaires has also been stimulated by the DSM-III and DSM-III-R. The descriptive and a-theoretical approach facilitated empirical research.

The Dutch Rorschach Society

The year in which the second edition of Exner's Volume 1 (Exner, 1986) appeared marked a turning point. Though Exner's work had been touched upon in some courses on psychodiagnosis prior to 1986, it was not until that year that a number of Dutch psychologists in different settings became actively involved with the Comprehensive System. The number of participants was small but the level of enthusiasm was high. In 1986 the Dutch Rorschach Society, devoted to work with the Comprehensive System in the Netherlands, was founded. In subsequent years members of the society schooled themselves in the System, and Anne Andronikof-Sanglade from France and John Exner from the United States came to the Netherlands to provide training. Exner provided a workshop on interpretation in 1989 and Andronikof-Sanglade has offered four introductory and interpretation courses since 1987. Additional courses have been provided by Dutch psychologists.

The principal activity to date of the Dutch Society has been furthering knowledge and understanding of the Comprehensive System through courses and local workshops. In addition members of the Society have played leading roles in the founding of the European Rorschach Association, an international scientific organization for psychologists in Europe who work with the Comprehensive System. Thirdly, the Society has been a formal and informal forum for the promotion of research with the Comprehensive System.

Research Projects

While studying Exner's Comprehensive System and realizing the complexity of the scoring system, a question arose concerning the interrater reliability. Derksen (1990) conducted an experiment while studying the Comprehensive System. The question was: is it possible to arrive at reasonable standards of reliability in scoring based solely upon the study of Exner's Volume I (1986)? Ten men and 10 women were administered the Rorschach test. Each protocol was independently scored by four psychologists who studied Exner's textbook. In weekly meetings Exner's book was studied and discussed and critical questions were raised. Scoring had been practiced on a small set of protocols scored by all four and had been discussed in the group. Each of the psychologists administered five of the protocols used in the experiment. The judgments were compared in pairs, which resulted in six pairs. The percentage agreement was established per pair. The codes that were selected for the comparison were those that produced the most unclarity during the training phase. These were developmental quality, pairs, reflections, all determinants, special scores, Z-score, form quality, and populars. The overall conclusion of this study was that the agreement between the psychologists scoring the Rorschach based on Exner's Volume I alone, was poor. The reliability appeared reasonable for the following categories: M, FM, chromatic color, pairs, Fr, DQ+, DQo, Z, and P. One of the causes for the poor reliability was attributed to the vague and unclear descriptions of the scoring categories. Our conclusion was that a reliable scoring of the Comprehensive System required training in administration and scoring and use of the workbook.

Panic Disorder with Agoraphobia

De Ruiter collected Rorschach Comprehensive System data from a small group (roughly 15%) of the 176 subjects participating in her doctoral dissertation research assessing the effectiveness of various behavioral treatments for patients suffering from panic disorder with agoraphobia (PDA) (de Ruiter, 1989). De Ruiter and Cohen (in press) used the Rorschach data to test a number of hypotheses derived by de Ruiter from Diamond's (1985) self psychology. Diamond asserted that PDA patients suffer from a developmental deficit in negative affect regulating capacity, surrounded by an elaborate constellation of defenses consisting of avoidance, repression, denial of negative affect and reaction formation against dependency needs. These defenses are seen as leading to an extensive constriction and rigidity of these patients' affective lives. WSumC and Afr were used to assess patients' resourceful affective activity. Lambda was used to assess avoidance of complexity and the general absence of food responses was treated as an indirect measure of denial of or reaction formation against dependency needs. The findings pointed to the presence of a highly avoidant information processing style (a remarkable 86% of protocols had Lambda > .99) and to a constricted affective life. The results were also consistent with the hypothesis of reaction formation against dependency needs. A valuable aspect of the research, in the authors' estimation, is that the CS was used to test hypotheses derived from psychodynamic theory.

Sleep Disorders

In his clinical practice with sleep-disturbed patients seen at a sleep center Cohen (1990) noted a high incidence of positive SCZI (Exner, 1986). In an exploratory study involving 95 sleep-disturbed patients and in which use was made of the revised, more stringent SCZI index (Exner, 1990) this finding was confirmed (Cohen, de Ruiter and Van Groningen, in preparation). No patients with an apnea syndrome, as assessed by nocturnal polysomnography, exhibited positive SCZI's. Of 35 patients with valid Rorschach protocols and for whom polysomnographic data are available, 7 patients were identified who scored positive on the SCZI. In all cases the positive SCZI was associated with the presence of patients' complaints pertaining to sleep. No patients presenting with snoring difficulties only – almost always a complaint of the partner and not of the patient – showed positive SCZI's.

The other major clinical indices of the Comprehensive System (the Depression Index and the Coping Deficit Index) did not differentiate between those patients presenting with only snoring complaints and those presenting with other sleep complaints nor did they discriminate between those manifesting clinical apnea and those not. The findings are consistent with the hypothesis that a subgroup of patients suffering from sleep disturbances for which there is no evident organic basis exhibit severe cognitive disturbances. Cohen (1990) has suggested that this subgroup may be characterized by ample resources in the social-emotional realm, which inhibits the development of major psychopathology. The study provided some findings supportive of this idea.

Transsexuality in Adolescence

Theories on transsexuality differ in the extent to which they attribute a role to psychopathology in the development of transsexuality and cross-gender identity. Transsexuals have been described on the one hand as exhibiting no more psychopathology than nonpatients (Fleming, Jones & Simons 1982; Mate-Kole, 1990) and on the other hand as suffering from borderline or other serious forms of psychopathology (Lothstein, 1984; Murray, 1985). To date studies have been carried out with gender identity disorder boys aged five to twelve (Tuber & Coates, 1989) and with adult transsexuals (e. g., Johnson & Hunt, 1990; Kuiper, 1991; Mate-Kole, Freschi & Robin, 1988; Murray, 1985). As far as we know, no reports have been published for studies with adolescent transsexuals. This group is particularly interesting because it has a shorter history of stigmatization and fewer ties to their original gender role than adult transsexuals.

At the University of Utrecht, where Cohen-Kettenis is engaged in long-term research on the development of gender identity, research is being carried out with adolescents presenting transsexuality. In 1986 Cohen, de Ruiter, and Cohen-Kettenis embarked on a study of Rorschach protocols gathered from a number of these adolescents. To date nearly 40 protocols have been collected. The principal research question concerns the presence of (serious) psychopathology in these patients. Preliminary analyses of the Rorschach protocols gathered to date indicate that as a group the Dutch adolescent transsexuals are characterized by indications of internal rage, by the absence of positive internal representations of relations with others, and by extreme absence of the need for closeness (90% of the protocols were "T-less"), severely disturbed reality testing, and mild thought disorders. These findings are in line with the findings by Murray (1985) who also found transsexuals to show high aggression, disturbed object relations and impaired reality testing. The researchers will conclude their data collection within a few months of the writing of this manuscript and expect to present their results shortly thereafter.

Multiple Sclerosis Patients

The premorbid personality of multiple sclerosis patients has been the subject of several investigations, but the empirical findings show many contradictions. Apart from the contradictions in the literature we can find a shared opinion that, although no specific personality type emerged, multiple sclerosis appears to be a disease which occurs predominantly in chronically anxious persons who had shown evidence of emotional and psychosexual immaturity (Lishman, 1987). Emotional stress is very disturbing for these people and so their tolerance for stress is low. A further finding was that multiple sclerosis patients tend to interpret the social environment atypically and not conforming to the socially shared opinions. Another finding concerns latent or manifest depression in these patients. These psychological characteristics make these patients probably vulnerable to emotionally traumatic experiences. This vulnerability can influence the course of multiple sclerosis.

Translated into the indices of the Comprehensive System we can expect five deviations in the structural summaries. The first will be a negative value for the D and adjusted D score. Especially the adjusted D we expect to be negative, because we can interpret the adjustment in these cases as a situation related adaptation of the patient to the disease multiple sclerosis itself. Furthermore we can expect a low X+% for the atypical interpretations of these patients. Also we can look at the X-% for the amount of distortions. The immature affects can be operationalized as CF+C being higher than FC. The depression index is expected to be higher than normal. Finally, we expect to find neurological deviations expressed in a high PSV.

Eighteen multiple sclerosis patients (7 men, 11 women) with a mean age of 50 years were administered the Rorschach test (Derksen & Bögels, 1990). To test the five hypotheses the means of the variables were compared to the American sample of 600 nonpatients adults (Exner, 1985). The statistical significance was tested by means of a t-test. The results indicated that although the D score is significantly lower (mean = −.88, $p < .05$, one tailed), the adjusted D score was not (mean = .06, ns). The vulnerability seems to be more state that trait dependent. The X+% was significantly lower (mean = .54, $p < .001$, one-tailed) and the X-% significantly higher (mean = .13, $p < .001$, one-tailed). Another finding in this respect was the low frequency of populars (mean = 1.28, $p < .001$, one-tailed).

Also interesting was a significantly low number of Detail responses (mean = 8.67, p < .001, one-tailed) and a high Dd (mean = 5.11, p .001, one-tailed). The multiple sclerosis group showed a mean FC:CF+C = 1.06:1.1, compared to Exner's sample with FC:CF+C = 3.87:2.19. This supported our hypothesis. The FC as well the CF responses were significantly lower than in protocols of nonpatients. The AFR was significantly lower (mean = .48, p < .001, one-tailed). Eleven of the 18 patients were ambitents. The DEPI index (mean = .56) was not high, so this hypothesis was not confirmed. The PSV (mean = .39, p < .001, one-tailed) was significantly higher. A more detailed report of this study, including the MMPI data of the subjects, is being prepared for publication.

Several research projects are still in progress. Over the past three years Rorschach protocols have been collected from patients in a psychotherapeutic community who have received a diagnosis of borderline personality organization (Kernberg 1984). Patients were tested at the intake, after one year of treatment and at the end of clinical treatment (mostly after two years). To date the results indicate that several subgroups of borderline patients can be formed based on the Rorschach data. Further, Rorschach protocols have recently been collected from 25 female university students in a test-retest study, and presentation of the findings is expected soon.

Epilogue

Although the activities of the Dutch Rorschach Society are promising and the research is taking shape, several problems accompany the introduction of the Comprehensive System in the Netherlands. One problem is the neo-positivistic climate in the social sciences. Among researchers in clinical psychology we can observe a dominant desire to measure components of behavior and experience by means of brief questionnaires. If, for instance, impulsivity is to be measured, this is preferably done by a series of self-rating questions directly based on research in this area. The idea is that the Rorschach as a technique is too elaborate and too much of a "broad band" method; the information about the individual that is produced is considered too general and lacking in specificity. These researchers also remark that the creation of the ten inkblots was too much an irrational process. "Why try make something of this old fashioned test; if you want to do something with perception, you better create new blots and determine precisely what components you need."

Of course this criticism is not totally without foundation. The evaluation of the Rorschach in clinical practice in the Netherlands, however, is usually completely different. Here the test is considered a rich instrument by means of which empirically based cognitive information can be gathered, as well as an observation instrument. For many clinicians administering the Rorschach is a practical experiment: the patient is confronted with a relatively unstructured assignment, and this gives the clinician a unique chance to observe the patient's behavior. For the psychodynamically oriented clinician the process of giving answers to the blots, in combination with the contents, provides numerous hypotheses regarding the psychodynamic constellation of the patient. For instance, ego functions such as defense mechanism's and reality testing can be assessed with the test.

In clinical practice the Rorschach also potentially gives information about the personality as a whole, instead of the information about details gathered with the questionnaires mentioned above, and about relations between different aspects of personality, such as cognitive functions and emotions. A self-report questionnaire merely organizes information directly given by the subject, and cannot, in principle, add very much to an elaborate clinical interview. In clinical practice the decisions one makes deal with complete, and thus complex, individuals, and there is need for information derived from instruments that cover this complexity. The Rorschach does.

An interesting point remains the fact that the Rorschach is essentially a perceptual test. The traits and characteristics of the individual that are inferred through use of the Comprehensive System are the result of the person's specific modes of perception. As far as we can see, a more profound theory about the relation between perception and personality is still to come.

Another matter of interest in the field of diagnostics is the increasing importance of the DSM-III-R classification. This point is particularly important with respect to daily collaboration with psychiatrists. What applies to the MMPI is especially true for the Rorschach: the data do not provide a DSM-III classification. The Rorschach results in an independent psychological picture of the individual. Much research has been done and will continue to be done in the future with the Rorschachs of patients with the same or different DSM-III diagnoses. For the SCZI index, for instance, this can lead to valid information, but on the whole this research compares apples and pears. If a DSM-III-R diagnosis tells you something about the exterior of a building, the Rorschach elaborates on the interior. In the domain of personality disorder research, Axis II of the DSM, we can expect more convergence of future findings because here the interpersonal behavior is the focus.

A major issue in the research in the Netherlands is the gathering of nonpatient and patient norms. Normal samples are especially difficult to obtain. For a representative sample in the Netherlands we need about 1,000 normals, and this entails a great deal of work and a lot of money. To get this far we need acceptance of the research project and financing of it by research funding organizations. Here we are confronted with the attitudes described above.

Apart from these difficulties, it is promising that the Dutch Rorschach society is starting with a databank this year. The databank provides representative samples of normals and clinical populations that clinicians can use to compare with their results. Every year the Dutch Rorschach Society organizes lectures about aspects of the Comprehensive System and training in scoring and interpretation. In the future we expect that no Dutch clinical psychologist will be able to disregard the Rorschach plates any longer.

Résumé

Cet article passe en revue le rôle qu'a joué et que joue encore le Rorschach au sein des activités que mènent les psychologues cliniciens hollandais. Dans les années 40 jusqu'au début des années 60, un rapport psychologique était considéré incomplet sans le Rorschach. Par contre, vers la fin des années 60, le Rorschach n'était plus pris au sérieux, au vu du climat scientifique empirique qui s'étendait rapidement. Cependant, l'utilisation du Rorschach subsistait dans des contextes cliniques. En 1988, un sondage révéls que parmi 195 participants, 60 % répondirent que le Rorschach avait été administré dans leur département ou leur institution. En 1986, la Société hollandaise de Rorschach, qui se voua à travailler avec le Système Synthétique dans les Pays-Bas, fut créée. Jusqu'à présent, l'activitè principale de cette Société a été de parfaire la connaisnance et la compréhension du Système Synthétique par des cours et des ateliers.

Plusieurs projets de recherche concernant le Système Synthétique sont résumés dans cet article. L'accord interjuges, obtenu chez des psychologues cotant le Rorschach sur la base du seul Volume I d'Exner, s'avérait faible. Une cotation fidèle du Système Synthétique requiert un entraînement à la fois au niveau de la passation, de la cotation et de l'utilisation du manuel.

Dans un échantillon de patients présentant des attaques de panique, le Rorschach démontre la présence d'un style de traitement de l'information fortement caractérisé par l'évitement; 86 % des protocoles ont un Lambda .99. Parmi 35 patients souffrant de troubles du sommeil, 7 présentent un score positif sur la SCZI. Quarante protocoles de Rorschach ont été réunis chez des adolescents transsexuels. Les analyses préliminaires indiquent que ces patients se caractérisent par des signes de rage interne, par une absence de représentations positives internalisées concernant leurs relations avec les autres, par une carence extrême des besoins de rapprochement, par une épreuve de réalité fortement atteinte et par des troubles de la pensée modérés. Une population de 18 patients souffrant de sclérose en plaques fut comparée à l'échantillon américain de 600 adultes non-patients; plusieurs points significatifs apparurent: un score D faible, X+% plus élevé, X−% plus élevé, une faible fréquence de banalités, peu de réponses de Détail, un Dd élevé, CF+C plus élevé que FC, AFR plus bas, PSV plus élevé etc. . . .

Les activités de la Société hollandaise de Rorschach et les problèmes qu'elle rencontre sont également discutés. Cette année, la Société commence une banque de données sur des échantillons non-représentatifs de populations normales et cliniques, que les cliniciens pourront utiliser à des fins de comparaison.

Resumen

En este artícule se presenta un resumen del rol que el Rorschach ha jugado y juega en las actividades de los psicólogos clinicos holandeses. Desde la década de los cuarenta hasta el comienzo de los sesenta, un informe psicológico sin la prueba de Rorschach era considerado incomplets. Al final de los sesenta, el Rorschach ya no era tomado en serio en el ambiente cientifico empírico que se desarrolló muy rápidamente. El Rorschach continuó siendo usado en los entornos clínicos. Una encuesta en 1988 encontró que, de 195 personas que respondieron a ella, el 60 % informó que el Rorschach se administraba en su departamento o institución de servicio. En 1986, se fundó la Sociedad Holandesa del Rorschach, dedicada a trabajar con el Sistema Comprensivo en los Paises Bajos. La actividad principal de la Sociedad hasta el presente consistió en incrementar el conocimiento y la comprensión del Sistema Comprensivo, a través de cursos y talleres locales. Varios proyectos de investigación, en base al Sistema Comprensivo, se resumen en este artículo. La confiabilidad interjueces, entre los psicólogos que codificaron el Rorschach en base al Volumen 1 de Exner, resultó baja. La codificación confiable del Sistema Comprensivo requiere entrenamiento en la administración y codificación, asi como el uso del manual. En una muestra de pacientes con pánico, el Rorschach señaló la presencia de un estilo muy evitativo en el procesamiento de información: 86 % de los protocolos tenían Lambda .99. De 35 pacientes con trastornos del sueño, se identificaron 7 con SCZI positive. Se reunieron 40 protocolos de Rorschach de adolescentes transexuales. Los análisis preliminares indican que estos pacientes se caracterizaron por manifestaciones de rabia interna, ausencia de representaciones internas positivas respecto a la relación con los otros y ausencia extrema de necesidad de cercanía, prueba de realidad severamente perturbada, y trastornos moderados del pensamiento. En un grupo de 18 pacientes con esclerósis múltiple, comparado con la muestra americana de 600 adultos no-pacientes, se dieron muchos hallazgos significativos: baja D y alta Dd, X+% más elevado, X-% más elevado, baja frecuencia de populares, CF+C mayor que FC, Afr inferior, PSV más elevada, etc. Se discuten las actividades y los problemas que encuentra la Sociedad Holandesa de Rorschach. Este año, la Sociedad ha iniciado una base de datos que provee muestras no representativas de poblaciones normales y clínicas, las cuales pueden ser usadas por el clínico para comparar sus resultados.

References

Bovenhoff, A., van Kemenade, H., de Ruiter, C., & Cohen, L. (1988). Rorschach-gebruik in Nederland: Verslag van een enquete. *De Psycholoog*, 23, 296–301.

Cohen, L. (1990). *Evidence of cognitive disorder in Rorschach protocols of chronic insomnia patients.* Paper presented at the 13th. International Congress of Rorschach and Projective Techniques. Paris: July.

Cronbach, L.J. (1949). Statistical methods applied to Rorschach scores: A review. *Psychological Bulletin*, 46, 393–409.

Derksen, J. (1990). *De ontwikkeling van de Rorschach tot een cognitieve test.* Paper presented at the Congress of Psychologists 1990. Amsterdam: October.

Derksen, J.J.L. & Bögels, T.J.P. (1990). *Rorschachgegevens van 18 MS-patiënten.* Poster presented at the Congress of Psychologists 1990. Amsterdam: October.

Diamond, D.B., (1985). Panic attacks, hypochondriasis and agoraphobia: A self-psychology formulation. *American Journal of Psychotherapy*, 39, 114–125.

Evers, A., & Zaal, J. (1979). De derde NIP-enquête onder testgebruikers. *De Psycholoog*, 14, 500–528.

Exner, J., (1985). *A Rorschach workbook for the comprehensive system.* Asheville: Rorschach Workshops.

Exner, J. (1986). *The Rorschach: A comprehensive system. Volume 1: Basic foundations.* New York: Wiley.

Exner, J. (1990). *A Rorschach workbook for the Comprehensive System.* (3rd ed.) Asheville: Rorschach Workshops.

Fleming, M., Jonas, D., & Simons, J. (1982). Preliminary results of Rorschach protocols of pre and post operative transsexuals. *Journal of Clinical Psychology*, 38, 408–415.

Johnson, S.L., & Hunt, D.D. (1990). The relation of male trans sexual typology to psychosocial adjustment. *Archives of Sexual Behavior*, 19, 349–360.

Kernberg, O. (1984). *Severe personality disorders: Psychotherapeutic strategies.* New Haven: Yale University Press.

Kuiper, A.J. (1991). *Transseksualiteit: Evaluatie van de geslachtsaanpassende behandeling* (Transsexuality: An evaluation of sex reassignment surgery). Doctoral dissertation, Free University, Amsterdam

Lishman, W.A. (1987). *Organic psychiatry: The psychological consequences of cerebral disorder.* Oxford: Blackwell Scientific Publications.

Mate-Kole, C., Freschi, M., & Robin, A. (1988). Aspects of psychiatric symptoms at different stages in treatment of transsexualism. *British Journal of Psychiatry*, 152, 550–553.

Murray, J.F. (1985). Borderline manifestations in the Rorschachs of male transsexuals. *Journal of Personality Assessment*, 49, 454–466.

Riemsdijk, J. van (1964). Op weg naar herwaardering van Rorschach test. *Nederlands Tijdschrift voor de Psychologie, 19*, 286–299.

Rorschach, H., (1921). *Psychodiagnostiek. Methodik und Ergebnisse eines wahrnehmungsdiagnostischen Experiments (Deutenlassen von Zufallsformen).* Bern: Bircher.

Ruiter, C. de (1989). *Psychological investigations into panic and agoraphobia.* Doctoral dissertation. University of Amsterdam.

Ruiter, C. de, & Cohen, L. (In press). Personality in panic disorder with agoraphobia: A Rorschach study. *Journal of Personality Assessment.*

Tuber, S., & Coates, S., (1989). Indices of psychopathology in Rorschachs of boys with severe gender identity disorders: A comparison with normal control subject. *Journal of Personality Assessment*, 53, 100–112.

Zeeuw, J. de (1986). *Persoonlijkheidsdiagnostiek volgens de vlekkenmethode.* Lisse: Swets & Zeitlinger.

The U.S. Rorschach Scene:
Integration and Elaboration

Philip Erdberg

Corte Madera, CA, USA

Two words describe the status of the Rorschach in the United States as we move into the 1990s. They are *integration* and *elaboration*. The integration is between structural and theoretically informed approaches to the test. The elaboration comes as researchers provide more and more data about various populations and clinical syndromes. This paper provides a survey of these trends over the past 5 years, surely among the most productive in American Rorschach history.

Integrating Theoretical and Structural Approaches

Two prize-winning works offer an excellent look at what is perhaps the most important trend in the U.S. Rorschach scene: the potential for an integration of empirical and theory-informed approaches to the test. These two approaches have traveled separate and sometimes adversarial paths in the past. The potential for their combination is a welcome one that promises to augment the instrument's yield.

Paul Lerner's recent (1991) book, *Psychoanalytic Theory and the Rorschach*, which won the 1991 Menninger Foundation Alumni Professional Writing Award, recognizes both the need for a systematic approach to the test and the importance of new developments in psychoanalytic theory. Extending the classic work of Rapaport, Gill, and Schafer (1968), he summarizes the developments in self psychology and object relations that have added significantly to psychoanalysis in the last two decades. He goes on to describe attempts to bring these new developments to the Rorschach, as illustrated in the work of Mayman (1977) and his group at the University of Michigan and Blatt and his colleagues at Yale University (see Blatt & Lerner, 1983; Blatt, Tuber, & Auerbach, 1990). His own "psychoanalytic diagnostic scheme" integrates Kernberg's (1970) organization of character pathology as well.

These approaches allow a more systematic approach to content, but they are premised on the assumption that Rorschach responses contain projective material. It is perhaps in the interpretation of content – how much of the Rorschach can be considered "projective" – that the empirical versus theoretical division has been most dramatic. In the past, theory-based Rorschachers and those advocating a structural approach often took diametrically opposing positions on this issue. Recently, the potential for integration seems more possible. Lerner, a leading proponent of a theory-based approach, confronts the issue directly, noting that "With content data, issues of reliability and validity cannot be disregarded; nonetheless, such issues need not exclude or minimize the clinical richness of the material" (p. 109).

It is fascinating to compare Lerner's comments to those of Exner (1989) in an article that won the annual Walter Klopfer Award of the Society for Personality Assessment. In this article, "Searching for Projection on the Rorschach," Exner cautions that many Rorschach answers do not involve projection but rather represent a simple "best fit" classification of the stimulus field. He argues that applying content analysis approaches which assume projection to such responses is erroneous. He suggests that the sort of projection which would make content analysis appropriate *may* occur when some kinds of answers – those involving minus form quality or embellished answers such as those attributing morbid, aggressive, or cooperative features to the percept – occur with greater than normative frequency. He comments as follows:

"... although the limited ambiguity of the blot fields plus the nature of the task do not encourage projection, they also do not prohibit or discourage the unique translations or embellishments which almost certainly have some projected properties. The ambiguity that does exist among the stimuli and the test situation permits some of the stronger needs, sets, attitudes, and so on of the subject to become influential in translating the stimuli and in the deciding to select those less common translations as responses to be delivered" (p. 527).

It is noteworthy, for example, that both Lerner and Exner suggest that human movement responses may be an area in which the kind of projection that would allow content analysis could occur. Exner's insistence on utilizing normative data to provide a baseline for such responses provides an important balance in the interpretation of a theoretically important class of answers that, in Lerner's words, allow the examiner "... to infer a vast array of structural and dynamic aspects of personality, including the capacity for perspective, the intensity of ideational activity, the availability of fantasy, the role of early self-experiences, the nature of self and object representations, and the quality of object relations" (p. 73).

More and more U.S. psychologists are drawing from both structural and theory-informed approaches in their thinking about the Rorschach. As the dialogue between proponents of these two traditions increases, the richness and accuracy of the test's yield will be substantially enhanced.

The other significant trend in the U.S. Rorschach scene recently has been the accumulation of increasing amounts of data about a variety of populations and clinical syndromes. Of particular note has been a focus on personality disorders. Other areas of significant interest have involved children and adolescents, older adults, and treatment planning and evaluation. It is not the purpose of this article to provide an exhaustive survey of these areas, but each will be described as a way of illustrating the level of elaboration that characterizes U.S. Rorschach research at present.

The Rorschach and Personality Disorder

The publication of the Third Edition of the *Diagnostic and Statistical Manual of Mental Disorders* (DSM-III) (American Psychiatric Association, 1980) made official what clinicians had known for a long time: that it is more helpful to describe a relatively large percentage of the clinical population in terms of deeply entrenched characterological difficulties than with the more dramatic psychopathological nomenclature whose roots are in the work of Bleuler and Kraepelin. A major contribution of *DSM-III* was its introduction of "Axis II," a part of the diagnostic nosology that gives specific recognition to the presence of these maladaptive characterological styles.

Axis II is divided into three clusters: Cluster A, which includes schizoid, schizotypal, and paranoid disorders; Cluster B, which includes borderline, narcissistic, histrionic, and antisocial disorders; and Cluster C, which includes avoidant, dependent, obsessive compulsive, and passive aggressive disorders. Although there is a good deal of overlap among these Axis II categories (Serban, Conte, & Plutchik, 1987; Frances, Clarkin, Gilmore, Hurt, & Brown, 1984), their introduction has been extraordinarily helpful in bringing greater focus and precision to an important area where description in the past was impressionistic at best. Rorschach researchers have been very much involved in the heightened attention that personality disorders have received. Of particular interest have been the areas of borderline and antisocial disorders.

Borderline Personality Disorders

A review of the empirical literature on borderline personality disorder (Gartner, Hurt, & Gartner, 1989) suggests that the Rorschach may be of utility in describing issues of thought disturbance, impulsivity, anger and suspiciousness, depression and anxiety, object relations, and self-focus for borderline personality disorders. This is consistent with a study by Exner (1986) that used the Rorschach to differentiate individuals with borderline personality disorder from those with schizotypal disorders or with schizophrenia.

Utilizing an object relations theory approach, Stuart, Westen, Lohr, Benjamin, Becker, Vorus, and Silk (1990) compared the Rorschach human responses of inpatient borderlines, inpatient depressives, and nonpatients and found that "... borderlines tend to understand human action as more highly motivated and human interaction as more malevolent in nature than do either depressives or normals. The data indicate that borderlines experience the object-relational world in a way that is fundamentally different from the way normals and depressives perceive it" (p. 297). Berg (1990) compared patients with borderline and narcissistic personality disorders in terms of ego functions. She found that the borderline disorders were characterized by less convergent reality testing and greater utilization of splitting defenses.

The area of borderline personality disorder continues to be one in which controversy abounds. The rapidly increasing body of Rorschach studies would seem to be of substantial value in the elucidation of this complex topic.

Antisocial Personality Disorders

Meloy and Gacono and their colleagues have utilized the Rorschach extensively in their work with the antisocial and narcissistic parts of the personality disorder spectrum. Their studies have provided a series of

Rorschach correlates for antisocial personalities that tend to support Meloy's (1988) conceptualization of the psychopath as a sadistic variant of narcissistic personality disorder whose psychological organization is characterized by the use of splitting and dissociative mechanisms.

Gacono, Meloy, and Heaven (1990) studied antisocial individuals who differed in their level of psychopathy as evaluated by a scale developed by Hare (1980). Highly psychopathic individuals were characterized by more reflection responses and more percepts containing a personal reference. Gacono (1990) used several Rorschach approaches that come from psychoanalytic theory as a way of studying the object relations and defensive operations of antisocial personality disorders. These included criteria developed by Kwawer (1980) for assessing borderline object relations and Rorschach scoring approaches suggested by Lerner and Lerner (1980) and Cooper and Arnow (1986) for the assessment of primitive defensive operations. The severe psychopaths in his sample were characterized by significantly greater suggestion of object relations organized at the borderline level of function.

The work of Meloy and Gacono provides a good example of an eclectic Rorschach approach, utilizing both empirical and theoretically based techniques, to describe a complex syndrome.

Children and Adolescents

The Rorschach has a long history in the assessment of children and adolescents. The 1982 publication of Comprehensive System normative data for children from 5 through 16 (Exner & Weiner) provided a framework from which researchers have operated for the last decade. Finch and his colleagues (e. g., Lipovsky, Finch, & Belter, 1989) have used the Rorschach extensively in the assessment of depression in children and adolescents. Another group that has provided extensive data on depression and thought disorder in adolescents includes Archer and his colleagues at Eastern Virginia Medical School (e. g., Archer & Gordon, 1988).

Russ has looked extensively at the Rorschach correlates of affective expression, primary process thinking, and creativity in children (Russ & Grossman-McKee, 1990; Russ, 1988). A study by Acklin (1990) continues the tradition of the test's utilization in school difficulties by investigating Rorschach characteristics of learning-disabled children. Galluci (1989) assessed gifted children with the Rorschach and concluded that "... intellectually superior children did process the Rorschach stimuli in a manner that was nonentrenched and reliably different from norms, but that these differences should not routinely be considered as indications of psychopathology" (p. 749).

The Rorschach provides a personality assessment instrument applicable across much of the life span. Its use with children and adolescents is of increasing value clinically, and the research implications of an instrument with an extensive developmental span are substantial.

The Elderly

At the other end of the developmental spectrum, several recent studies have extended the work of Rorschach (1921/1942), Klopfer (1946), and Ames and her colleagues (Ames, Metraux, Rodell, & Walker, 1973) in using the test to describe older adults. Peterson (1991) has suggested that methodological flaws in Ames' approach may have restricted the potential richness of the records she obtained and led her to describe the elderly as more inflexible and impoverished than is actually the case.

Consistent with this concern and a similar one expressed by Reichlin (1984), Gross, Newton, and Brooks (1990) studied healthy, community-dwelling older adults. They found little suggestion that Rorschach scores were influenced by age in this group. Their conclusion suggests that it may be moderator variables – medical, emotional, and psychosocial impairments – frequently associated with the elderly and not the aging process itself that accounts for the Rorschach changes that have previously been noted. They conclude that "Those who manifest these impairments show personality changes that are reflected in their Rorschach scores. It may be that those older adults who are fortunate enough to escape these problems and who live in their own homes can be expected to retain the personality characteristics of their younger years" (pp. 341–342).

As older adults make up a larger percentage of the population and become more frequent recipients of mental health services, the elaboration of normative data for this group becomes increasingly important. Rorschach's original generalization that the aging process accounted for the lowered levels of responsiveness and accuracy he saw with his older patients would now appear to be oversimplistic. The multivariate approaches that characterize current research will help to make our understanding of this important group more precise.

Treatment Planning and Evaluation

The Rorschach plays an important role in planning and evaluating psychological treatment. Two recent studies (Gerstle, Geary, Himmelstein, & Reller-Geary, 1988; LaBarbera & Cornsweet, 1985) have looked at the Rorschach correlates of treatment outcome for children in inpatient settings. A study by Weiner and Exner (1991) provides a highly detailed look at the ways that the Rorschach can be utilized in assessing the changes that occur during psychotherapy. Presenting data from outpatient psychotherapy patients tested at four points during or after treatment, they found differing change patterns for those involved in long-term versus short-term therapy. Although they caution that their findings are preliminary and not definitive, the study strongly supports the Rorschach's utility in describing the sorts of changes – in stress tolerance, affective modulation, interpersonal comfort, accurate ideation, and self-awareness – that the psychotherapy research literature suggests should happen in the course of treatment.

Instruments that can provide sequential assessment of progress will become increasingly important in a health-services delivery climate that emphasizes the need for accurate treatment planning, brief therapy, and ongoing monitoring of intervention. The Rorschach's resurgence may be further strengthened by its substantial value in these areas.

Conclusion

The last 5 years have been extraordinarily active ones for the Rorschach in the U.S. The accumulation of elaborated data about a variety of populations, syndromes, and interventions provides an increasingly solid framework for clinical work. And the potential for integration of structural and theory-based approaches will bring even greater richness to this remarkable instrument's interpretive yield.

Résumé

Récemment, la scène du Rorschach aux Etats-Unis s'est caractérisée par deux tendances: l'intégration et l'élaboration. L'intégration apparaît dans les efforts croissants qui visent à combiner les approches structurales/empiriques du test avec celles dérivées d'une théorie de la personnalité. L'élaboration se produit à mesure que les chercheurs accumulent des données relatives à une diversité de populations cliniquement importantes, de syndromes et de procédures d'intervention.

Deux ouvrages récents (Lerner, 1991; Exner, 1989) illustrent à merveille l'émergence d'une double approche de l'interprétation du Rorschach, à la fois structurale et théoriquement fondée. L'ouvrage de Lerner, tout en insistant sur une approche plus systématique des contenus, suppose aussi que la production de percepts au Rorschach renvoie à la projection. L'étude d'Exner examine attentivement si le genre de projection qui sous-tend l'analyse de contenus se produit réellement au Rorschach. Il en conclut que celle-ci *peut* intervenir lorsque des réponses à connotation morbide, agressive ou coopérative se produisent à une fréquence plus élevée que la normale. Son approche pourrait se prêter à une quantification des variables "projectives", nouveauté qui rendrait ce domaine plus ouvert à la recherche empirique.

La deuxième tendance significative dans les recherches américaines sur le Rorschach a été l'accumulation de données plus minutieuses, concernant une diversité de populations cliniquement importantes, de syndromes et de traitements. Sans être un résumé exhaustif, le présent exposé décrit des réalisations concernant les troubles de la personnalité, les enfants et les adolescents, les adultes plus âgés et les évaluations de traitement.

Ainsi, l'on repère un intérêt croissant dans l'utilisation du Rorschach avec des troubles de la personnalité borderline. Dans ce contexte, la valeur du test réside dans la description des troubles de la pensée, de l'impulsivité, de l'affect, des relations d'objet et de la psychologie du self. Les travaux de Meloy, Gacono et leurs collègues (par exemple, Meloy, 1988; Gacono, Meloy, & Heaven, 1990) ont fourni une compréhension théorique et des données Rorschach étendues au sujet de la personnalité antisociale. Leurs travaux sur ce groupe présentent une série de corrélats au Rorschach, de plus en plus riche.

Les progrès dans l'utilisation du Rorschach avec des enfants et des adolescents bénéficièrent de la publication des données normatives du

Système Synthétique pour les sujets de cinq à seize ans. Passablement d'intérêt semble être suscité par les enfants et les adolescents dans des contextes hospitaliers. Par ailleurs, la longue tradition d'utilisation du test dans le domaine scolaire se poursuit, avec une insistance croissante sur les troubles d'apprentissage et les enfants doués.

De nouvelles orientations dans l'étude Rorschach des personnes âgées ont mis en lumière le domaine du vieillissement normal, ce qui représente un changement de cap par rapport aux travaux antérieurs, qui semblent avoir étudié davantage des groupes plus atteints sur le plan médical et social. En l'absence de telles difficultés, il semblerait que les personnes âgées, qui demeurent intégrées à leur communauté, ne présentent pas de changements significatifs au Rorschach en rapport avec le vieillissement normal.

Enfin, plusieurs études (par exemple, Weiner & Exner, 1991; LaBarbera & Cornsweet, 1985) suggèrent que le Rorschach peut s'avérer un outil précieux pour la planification du traitement et pour l'évaluation des changements en rapport avec ce dernier.

Resumen

El escenario reciente del Rorschach en los Estados Unidos se ha caracterizado por dos tendencias: integración y elaboración. La integración se presenta en los ensayos crecientes por combinar los enfoques empírico-estructurales con aquellos basados en la teoría de la personalidad. La elaboración ocurre a medida que los investigadores acumulan más datos acerca de una variedad de poblaciones, sindromes y procesos de intervención clínicamente importantes.

Dos trabajos recientes (Lerner, 1991; Exner, 1989) constituyen excelentes ejemplos del interés emergente en utilizar ambos enfoques, el estructural y el basado en teorías, en la interpretación del Rorschach. El trabajo de Lerner, al enfatizar un estudio más sistemático del contenido, asume que la producción de los perceptos en el Rorschach involucra la proyección. El estudio de Exner observa con atención si se presenta en el Rorschach el tipo de proyección que permitiría el análisis del contenido. Este último autor concluye que ello *puede* ocurrir, cuando se presentan respuestas que contienen elaboraciones mórbidas, agresivas o cooperativas, en una frecuencia mayor a la esperada de acuerdo a los datos normativos. Su enfoque permitiría la cuantificación de las variables "proyectivas", un desarrollo que podría hacer a esta área más accesible a la investigación empírica.

La segunda tendencia significativa en los estudios recientes con el Rorschach en los Estados Unidos, ha sido la acumulación de datos más elaborados acerca de varias poblaciones, síndromes y enfoques de tratamiento clínicamente importantes. Aunque no constituye un resumen exhaustivo, este trabajo describe los progresos que se han hecho en cuanto a los trastornos de la personalidad, niños y adolescentes, tercera edad, y evaluación de tratamiento.

Hay un interés creciente en la utilización del Rorschach con el trastorno borderline de la personalidad. La prueba podría ser de utilidad en la descripción de los problemas de pensamiento, impulsividad, afecto, relaciones de objeto y psicología del sí mismo. El trabajo de Meloy, Gacono y sus colaboradores (e. g. Meloy, 1988; Gacono, Meloy y Heaven, 1990) ha aportado una comprensión teórica amplia y datos en el Rorschach acerca del trastorno antisocial de la personalidad. Su trabajo presenta una serie, cada vez más elaborada, de correlatos en el Rorschach para este grupo.

El progreso en la utilización de Rorschach con niños y adolescentes fué ayudado por la publicación de los datos normativos del Sistema Comprensivo (Exner & Weiner, 1982), para edades que van de los cinco a los dieciseis años. Ha habido un interés considerable en niños y adolescentes hospitalizados. Continúa la larga tradición en la utilización del test en entornos escolares, con un énfasis creciente en las dificultades de aprendizaje y los niños superdotados.

Las nuevas direcciones en el estudio de la tercera edad a través del Rorschach, han llamado más la atención acerca del proceso normal de envejecimiento; ello implica un cambio respecto a los trabajos anteriores, que habian estudiado grupos más deteriorados, desde el punto de vista médico y psicosocial. En ausencia de tales dificultades, pareciera que las personas de la tercera edad, que habitan en la comunidad, no demuestran cambios significativos en el Rorschach como producto del proceso normal de envejecimiento.

Finalmente, una variedad de estudios (e. g. Weiner y Exner, 1991; La-Barbera y Cornsweet, 1985) sugieren que el Rorschach puede ser de considerable utilidad en la planificación del tratamiento y en la evaluación de los cambios producidos por la intervención.

References

Acklin, M. (1990). Personality dimensions in two types of learning-disabled children: A Rorschach Study. *Journal of Personality Assessment, 54*, 62–77.

American Psychiatric Association. (1980). *Diagnostic and statistical manual of mental disorders* (3rd ed.). Washington, DC: Author.

Ames, L. B., Metraux, R. W. Rodell, J. L., & Walker, R. N. (1973). *Rorschach responses in old age* (2nd ed.). New York: Brunner-Mazel.

Archer, R. P., & Gordon, R. (1988). MMPI and Rorschach indices of schizophrenic and depressive diagnoses among adolescent inpatients. *Journal of Personality Assessment, 52*, 276–287.

Berg, J. (1990). Differentiating ego functions of borderline and narcissistic personalities. *Journal of Personality Assessment, 55*, 537–548.

Blatt, S., & Lerner, H. (1983). The psychological assessment of object representation. *Journal of Personality Assessment, 47*, 7–28.

Blatt, S., Tuber, S., & Auerbach, J. (1990). Representation of interpersonal interactions on the Rorschach and level of psychopathology. *Journal of Personality Assessment, 54*, 711–728.

Cooper, S., & Arnow, D. (1986). An object relations view of the borderline defense: A Rorschach analysis. In M. Kissen (Ed.), *Assessing object relations phenomena* (pp. 143–171). Madison, CT: International Universities Press.

Exner, J. E. (1986). Some Rorschach data comparing schizophrenics with borderline and schizotypal personality disorders. *Journal of Personality Assessment, 50*, 455–471.

Exner, J. E. (1989). Searching for projection on the Rorschach. *Journal of Personality Assessment, 53*, 520–536.

Exner, J. E., & Weiner, I. B. (1982). *The Rorschach: A comprehensive system. Volume 3: Assessment of children and adolescents.* New York: Wiley.

Frances, A., Clarkin, J., Gilmore, M. Hurt, S., & Brown, R. (1984). Reliability of criteria for borderline personality disorder: A comparison of DSM-III and the diagnostic interview of borderline patients. *American Journal of Psychiatry, 141*, 1080–1084.

Gacono, C. (1990). An empirical study of object relations and defensive operations in antisocial personality disorder. *Journal of Personality Assessment, 54*, 589–600.

Gacono, C., Meloy, J. R., & Heaven, T. (1990). A Rorschach investigation of narcissism and hysteria in antisocial personality. *Journal of Personality Assessment, 55*, 270–279.

Galluci, N. T. (1989). Personality assessment with children of superior intelligence: Divergence versus psychopathology. *Journal of Personality Assessment, 53*, 749–760.

Gartner, J., Hurt, S., & Gartner, A. (1989). Psychological test signs of borderline personality disorder: A review of the empirical literature. *Journal of Personality Assessment, 53*, 423–441.

Gerstle, R. M., Geary, D. C., Himmelstein, P., & Reller-Geary, L. (1988). Rorschach predictors of therapeutic outcome for inpatient treatment of children: A proactive study. *Journal of Clinical Psychology, 44,* 277–280.

Hare, R. (1980). A research scale for the assessment of psychopathy in criminal populations. *Personality and Individual Differences, 1,* 111–119,

Kernberg, O. (1970). A psychoanalytic classification of character pathology. *Journal of the American Psychoanalytic Association, 18,* 800–822.

Klopfer, W. G. (1946). Personality measures of old age. *Rorschach Research Exchange, 10,* 145–166.

Kwawer, J. (1980). Primitive interpersonal modes, borderline phenomena and Rorschach content. In J. Kwawer, A. Sugarman, P. Lerner, & H. Lerner (Eds.), *Borderline phenomena and the Rorschach test* (pp. 89–105). New York: International Universities Press.

LaBarbera, J. D., & Cornsweet, C. (1985). Rorschach predictors of therapeutic outcome in a child psychiatric inpatient service. *Journal of Personality Assessment, 49,* 120–124.

Lerner, P., & Lerner, H. (1980). Rorschach assessment of primitive defenses in borderline personality structure. In J. Kwawer, A. Sugarman, P. Lerner, & H. Lerner (Eds.), *Borderline phenomena and the Rorschach test* (pp. 257–274). New York: International Universities Press.

Lerner, P. M. (1991). *Psychoanalytic theory and the Rorschach.* Hillsdale, NJ: Analytic Press.

Lipovsky, J., Finch, A. J., & Belter, R. (1989). Assessment of depression in adolescents: Objective and projective measures. *Journal of Personality Assessment, 53,* 449–458.

Mayman, M. (1977). A multi-dimensional view of the Rorschach movement response. In M. Rickers-Ovsiankina (Ed.), *Rorschach psychology* (pp. 229–250). Huntington, NY: Krieger.

Meloy, J. R. (1988). *The psychopathic mind: Origins, dynamics, and treatment.* Northvale, NJ: Aronson.

Peterson, C. (1991). Reminiscence, retirement, and Rorschach responses in old age. *Journal of Personality Assessment, 57,* 531–536.

Rapaport, D., Gill, M., & Schafer, R. (1968). *Diagnostic psychological testing* (rev. ed.). New York: International Universities Press.

Reichlin, R. E. (1984). Current perspectives on Rorschach performance among older adults. *Journal of Personality Assessment, 48,* 71–81.

Rorschach, H. (1921). *Psychodiagnostik.* Bern: Bircher. (English translation, Bern: Hans Huber, 1942).

Russ, S. (1988). Primary process thinking on the Rorschach, divergent thinking, and coping in children. *Journal of Personality Assessment, 52,* 539–548.

Serban, G., Conte, H., & Plutchik, R. (1987). Borderline and schizotypal personality disorders: Mutually exclusive or overlapping? *Journal of Personality Assessment, 51,* 15–22.

Stuart, J., Westen, D., Lohr, N., Benjamin, J. Becker, S., Vorus, N., & Silk, K. (1990). Object relations in borderlines, depressives, and normals: An examination of human responses on the Rorschach. *Journal of Personality Assessment, 55,* 296–318.

Weiner, I. B., & Exner, J. E. (1991). Rorschach changes in long-term and short-term psychotherapy. *Journal of Personality Assessment, 56,* 453–465.